POPE PAUL VI

AND HIS QUEST FOR PEACE:
1963-1978

*A Commentary on the New Year's
Peace Messages of Paul VI: 1968-1978:*

VOLUME TWO:
"If You Want Peace..."

REV JOHN F TUOHEY, PhD

Olympus Story House
www.olympusstoryhouse.com

CONTENTS
VOLUME TWO

CONTENTS
VOLUME ONE

Paul VI: 1963- 1978

DEDICATION

This work is dedicated to my Mother and Dad, my siblings and their spouses: Mary Pat and Stephen, Chris and Christy; my nieces and nephews of all generations: Along the Pavelka line with spouses and the next generation: Stefanie and Todd with Brynn & Kayden; Marty with Mackenzie; Joe and Annie with Jackson & Adeline. Along the Tuohey line: Patrick & Dana.

Without their unconditional love, bottomless patience and unlimited support and encouragement this project would truly never have come to fruition. Thank you!

ACKNOWLEDGMENTS

I want to acknowledge the support, patience and encouragement of my family in this project. I want to thank the monks at St Mary' monastery where I am an Oblate, as wells as the Benedictine nuns of St Scholastica Priory in Petersham, MA. Their hospitality made a world of difference as I worked on these books. I want to single out Br. Isidore who is both Guest Master and Librarian. The monastery has a wonderful collection of books by and about Paul VI which he generously shared. Several of the works on Paul VI in their library did not show up in any of my literature searches or bibliographies of other works. Having English translations of some of his own works when archbishop of Milan was especially helpful. I am also indebted to the Boston College Libraries where I found an excellent collection for my research, and the assistance of Chris Strauber in compiling a bibliography for me in the early stages of my research. The staff of the Library at Elms College, the local Catholic college here in the diocese has also been helpful, as has been the staff of the Westfield Athenaeum, as our local library is called, whose interlibrary service was very helpful in tracking books down. John Alonzo Dick, a fellow *alum* from the Katholieke Universiteit Leuven, Louvain, Belgium, was very helpful reading my early texts and giving me pointers as well as access to his own work on Archbishop Jean Jadot, Paul VI's nuncio in the US during the last five years of his papacy. Finally, I want to thank all the wonderful people who so patiently listened to me getting carried away with my enthusiasm for my project. And of course, I readily acknowledge the watchful eye of the Saint himself. I trust he approves of what I have written about him.

INTRODUCTION TO VOLUME 2

*"Long enough have I been dwelling with
those who hate peace. I am for peace."*
PSALM 120:6

This present work is Volume 2 of *Pope Paul VI and his Quest for World Peace 1963-1978*. In Volume 1, "Never Again War," I explored his 1965 Address to the United Nations General Assembly, his work with the Second Vatican Council's defining of a "new attitude towards war" and subsequent changes to Church teaching, and his unique relationship with US President Lyndon Johnson as well as his opposition to the Vietnam War and the role he played in bringing it to an end.

The focus of this second volume is his enduring vision of and the pathways to peace articulated in his annual *New Year's Day Peace Messages*. With his first *Message* of January 1, 1968, he defines the purpose of what is truly a new genre of papal teaching: to give greater insight into the substance of an "exact idea of peace." In his 1972 *Message* he further writes that, "it is of extreme importance" to have such an exact idea. His final *Message* in 1978, one that he seems to have intuited would be his last, he brings the collection full circle by writing it is the task of all humanity to bring a vision of an authentic and genuine peace to our prayer and contemplation that together we might, as he called upon the UN to do in 1965, "Go forward!" in our common quest for world peace. "Going forward" towards peace is our common and necessary task even if it seems at times, as referenced in Psalm 120 above, we find ourselves surrounded by those who, by their warlike rhetoric and/or actions, seem to hate peace.

In Part One of this volume, two distinct and we might even say irreconcilable ways of thinking about and pursuing peace are explored. Chapter 1 will explore the historical development and influence of the dominant approach: "If you want peace, prepare for war." Chapter 2 will explore the theological approach that influenced the thinking and vison of Paul VI. We see this theological foundation demonstrated in the historical narrative presented in Volume 1.

Part Two is devoted to presenting a commentary on the theme of each annual *Message*, each with its own insightful response or "tagline" we might say to the ancient formula "If you want peace..." Chapter 3 will examine the years 1968-1973, followed by Chapter 4 examining years 1974-1978. A conclusion fitting for both Volumes 1 and 2 of *Pope Paul VI and his Quest for Peace* then follows.

It is important to note from the start that Paul VI does not make mention of any particular global conflict in these annual *Messages*. He makes no mention, one might think somewhat surprisingly, of Vietnam. Nor does he reference to any of the *coup d'etats* taking place during his fifteen-year papacy.[1] His aim is not to address specific events, but to articulate a vision of what he calls a "genuine," an "authentic" peace, and the pathways to it. His purpose is to offer clarity as to what is required of us if we want peace, not to comment on the conflicts of his time. As he explains in his 1970 *Message*, "It is not Our duty to pass judgment on the disputes still in progress between nations, races, tribes, and social classes. But it is Our mission to cast the word 'Peace' into the midst of men at strife with one another." By taking this approach his *Messages* can be said to survive and go past their own particular moment in time. His insights possess a timeless relevance that can help shape our thinking about peace even to today.

Having said this, because the Vietnam War was of particular concern to him, of such consequence in his relationship with Lyndon Johnson, and a conflict in which he was ultimately able to play an important role in bringing the conflict to the beginning of its end, described in detail in Chapter 6 of Volume 1, I will introduce each year with a brief overview of events unfolding in Southeast Asia. Even if Paul VI himself does not address Vietnam in these *Peace Messages*, his outspoken opposition to the war and his role in bringing about the

Paris Peace Talks which ultimately, if not belatedly, brought an end to the war during his lifetime, I believe it is helpful to put each year's *Peace Message* in that historical context.

In writing this commentary as a second volume to a larger work, I have come to the conclusion that, as important as his more formal writings are to is message of peace: we think here of his declaration of "development" as the new name for peace in his 1967 encyclical *Populorum Progressio*, and his adamant rejection of violence in his 1975 Apostolic Exhortation *Evangelii Nuntiandi* explored in some detail in Volume 1, these eleven *New Year's Peace Messages* as a single body of work make up what can rightfully be recognized as his most important contribution to his legacy as a pope who dedicated his papacy to the pursuit of world peace. They deserve, as they find here, their own presentation, exploration, and commentary. Volume 2 can be seen standing on its own, written in anticipation we can say of the 60th anniversary of Paul VI initiating this annual practice to be celebrated January 1, 2028, a practice that has been continued by his successors.

It is unfortunate, at least as I could find, that there are no previously published works devoted to providing a commentary on or even publishing an edited collection of this body of Paul VI's writings. This text is my singular attempt to bring these *Peace Messages* once again to our attention for our study and appreciation and offering a commentary that integrates them with his other writings and each other, as well as the broader Catholic Social Justice tradition. I apologize that these commentaries cannot begin to capture the full flavor and love of peace of this pope. No commentary can take the place of the pope's own words, especially a pope as gifted and as articulate as this one. Perhaps you will decide to read these *Messages* yourself. They are brief, concise, and most beautifully written. They are at times poetic, at times using liturgical language, as he did in his 1965 UN speech. They are at times prophetic in a way similar to his 1971 Apostolic Letter *Octogesima Adveniens* "On the 80th Anniversary" (of *Rerum Novarum*). They always and without fail possess and convey a profound optimism that a world at peace is not impossible. "Difficult," he will allow, "but not impossible."

PART ONE

TO LINK OR NOT TO LINK
The Relationship of War to Peace

1
The Historical Role of War in Seeking Peace

*"Never reach out your hand unless
you're willing to extend an arm."*
PAUL VI

INTRODUCTION

THROUGHOUT HUMAN HISTORY THERE HAVE BEEN A VARIETY OF TAGLINES TO COMPLETE the formula, "If you want peace..." The most influential to today is "prepare for war:" "If you want peace, prepare for war." Of all the truisms handed down throughout history this one certainly has one of the longest of shelf lives. As will be seen in this Chapter there are other taglines that have connected war to the pursuit of peace, explicitly expressed and/or demonstrated by national behavior. What they have in common is the conviction that there is an intimate relationship between peace and war. From the 4th century BC until today, the prevailing political and military assumption is that if you want peace, conflict and war have something to do with obtaining it.

This present chapter will provide a brief history of the relationship between peace and war as expressed in the various taglines to "If you want peace..." This overview will provide the context and contrast for the focus of Chapter 2 and its examination of the theological foundations from which Paul VI will draw his taglines as the pathway to peace. We begin first with an issue of importance both to the historical evolution of the formula "If you want peace..." and Paul VI's insights: What does it mean to "want" peace, and what is the "peace" we want?

"WANTING" PEACE AND WANTING "PEACE"

A formula we can infer from Paul VI's 1974 *Peace Message* relevant to this discussion is, "If you want peace, want peace." There are two ways of interpreting this phrasing that capture both the historical evolution of the formula as well as Paul VI's insights. The first interpretation is to emphasize the "wanting:" "If you _want_ peace, _want_ peace." It is not enough to hope for or wish for peace. He will on numerous occasions emphasize that we must not look upon peace as some wistful utopia. There must be a true and sincere desire that genuine peace become a reality. Only a deep, heart-felt desire, he reminds us, can motivate humanity to engage in the works and sacrifices necessary to achieve peace, as well as to keep an optimism for peace alive. As he is quoted by friend Jean Guitton, "Peace is indeed difficult...it is very difficult, extremely difficult. All the same as I said just now, it is not impossible."[2] The measure of our desire for peace must be greater than the difficulty of achieving it.

The necessity of being truly committed to wanting peace is also illustrated by his insistence on nonviolence in the pursuit of justice. A hallmark of Paul VI's theology is that one should be willing to suffer for the sake and in the pursuit of justice.[3] We do not engage in physical fighting for justice, and neither do we disengage from its pursuit. Instead, we must be ready to suffer for the sake of justice as we work for it with such nonviolent methods as boycotts, strikes, protests and the like. This is illustrated most clearly in his _Addresses_ in Columbia in 1968 and in his 1975 Apostolic Exhortation _Evangelii Nuntiandi_, "In Proclaiming the Gospel."[4]

The second way of interpreting this tagline central to understanding Paul VI is to place emphasis on what is wanted: "If you want _peace_, want _peace_." Humanity cannot have a vague, ill-defined notion of peace. We need to know exactly what it is we want when we say we want peace. In his 1972 _Peace Message_ he writes that it is "of extreme important to have an exact idea of Peace." Having an "authentic conception is indispensable." Knowing precisely what we want is the only way we can gain insight into how to possess it. As will be seen in this and the following chapter, whatever the sincerity and genuineness of one's desire for peace, "If we want peace, we need to want genuine peace." How we understand peace will set the stage for how it will be pursued.

We need not nor should we call into question the sincerity of those who have a different understanding and conception of peace than that Paul VI will put forward in these annual *Peace Messages*. The issue is not the sincerity of a desire for peace, but of the type and kind of peace wanted.

PEACE AS STABILITY & SECURITY

From a national security perspective peace has historically been and largely remains so today as that tranquility found in a stable and ordered social environment, one in which everyone knows his and her place, duties and obligations. It is this stability and order that provides a sense and assurance of security, a sense of living in peace, what Paul VI will refer to as the "pretense" of peace. Whereas most people would presumably not argue with this there is a caveat that may be underappreciated, a caveat well appreciated by Paul VI and historians such as Ali Parchami.[5] If peace is a matter of social stability and order, it will be necessary that there be some manner of enforcing and maintaining that stability. This can lead to what Parchami describes as a "loose interpretation" of peace, loose in the sense that it grants a degree of latitude and license as to by whom and how to achieve and preserve it. It often happens that those who benefit most from the established social order, from "peace," are able to exercise the threat or use of force to preserve it. Prime examples Parchami gives of such a "loose interpretation of peace" are the periods of peace known as the *Pax Romana*, the Peace of Rome, and the *Pax Britannica*, the Peace of Britain.

PAX ROMANA

The period known as the *Pax Romana* began with Ceasar Agustus in 27 BC and continued for some 200 years, well after the birth of Jesus of Nazareth, the "Prince of Peace." (Isaiah,9,6) The peace of that period was a political and commercial stability that allowed the citizens of the Roman Empire to live relatively ordered and secure lives: to live in an Empire of peace. This *Pax Romana* was not enjoyed by non-citizens within the empire, nor was it enjoyed by those upon whose enslavement political and economic stability greatly depended. It was also during this period that the empire was expanding, and not by the type of rhetorical persuasion for which the Roman Senate was renowned but through military conquest. It cannot be said that the peoples conquered in that expansion of the empire enjoyed any of the peace of the empire. The *Pax Romana*, as Parchami points out, was ruthlessly imposed on some by the dominance of a ruling elite. Political and economic stability, a type and kind of peace, required the imposing of order on others by those who benefited from it.

An example of the empire's approach to peace is the rebellion in Roman occupied Israel in AD 66 that resulted in the destruction of the Temple in Jerusalem in AD 70.[6] The most egregious example might be said to be Rome's response to the Spartacus Rebellion in 71 BC. In its failed aftermath 6,000 enslaved Spartans were crucified along the 400-mile Appian way, the principle commercial route connecting Rome to the Port of Brindisi. Whereas Jesus and the thieves crucified with him were taken down from their crosses in deference to the Sabbath (John 19,31-34), those crucified on the Appian Way had neither their legs broken, nor their hearts pierced to assure a quick death. They were simply left to die slowly and in agony, their bodies left on the crosses exposed to the elements of animals and weather. Being the most important commercial route of the time, these crucifixions were meant not to punish but rather to terrorize, to inject fear into the hearts of anyone travelling along the way.[7] It worked. There were no further attempts by those enslaved to achieve freedom within the empire, 30% of whom were native Italians. Hence we have the *Pax Romana*: the "Peace of *Rome*," not "Peace of the Roman Empire.

In a similar way the *Pax Britannica* of the British Empire during the Victorian Era of 1820-1914 (Queen Victoria reigned from 1837-1901) was a time of political and economic stability enjoyed by some in *Britain* at the time, not a peace of the *British Empire*. As in the Roman Empire peace meant the security of a ruling aristocratic elite who enjoyed among themselves their perceived superiority over other cultures and peoples. Those of the lesser classes and especially those of conquered territories of the Empire had this peace at times ruthlessly imposed on them. This peace was threatened in Britain, as it would be in the US, by the formation of Trade Unions seeking to protect workers from the dangerous and unhealthy working conditions that accompanied the advent of the industrial revolution. Unions were criminalized in Britian until 1867. [8] Britain's navy helped preserve the empire's political and economic stability by ensuring its domination of the world's oceans, a point of contention with Pope Benedict XV's call for freedom of the seas in his *Peace Note* of 1917. National aspirations in Ireland and India were not tolerated, the *Pax Britannia* being violently imposed to preserve an empire over which the sun never went down.[9] As with the *Pax Romana*, the *Pax Britannica* was grounded in a "loose interpretation" of a peace and how to preserve it.

Parshami references also a similar *Pax Americana*. Reflecting Paul VI's interest in the civil rights movement in the US, particularly his meeting and great respect for the Rev. Dr. Martin Luther King, Jr. I would like to suggest here as examples of the "Peace of America" South Carolina's 1860 "Articles of Succession" from the Union. These articles clearly articulate the Southern enslaving state's perceived threat to their economies from the failure of Northern free states to enforce the Fugitive Slave Act of 1850 requiring the return of enslaved persons who had fled to freedom in the North. The South also feared the increasing hostility in the North towards the US Constitution's "Three-fifths Clause" which allowed the Southern enslaving states to count those enslaved as three-fifths of a person for the apportionment of representatives in the US Congress. Allowing the enslaved to count towards representation in Congress is an example of a *Pax Americana* as it ensured the preservation of the political power of states whose enslaved population greatly outnumbered the free White population.

The pervasiveness of *de-facto* apartheid and the discrimination and violence Black Americans experienced during the Jim Crow days are examples in our own nation of the imposition of a loose interpretation of peace in the service of a privileged class. Upon his election in 1913 President Woodrow Wilson re-segregated the US

Civil Service. This segregation greatly benefited the White majority population while bringing about economic hardships among minority civil servants, hardships that continue to reverberate today. I would also note the violence that accompanied the Civil Rights Movement in the 1960's. The most brutal and ultimately consequential was seen on March 7, 1965, when police, state troopers, and even ordinary citizens violently attacked civil rights marchers attempting to cross the Edmund Pettus Bridge in Selma, Alabama. As if to confirm the notion of "poetic justice," just four months later, July 2, 1965, as a direct result of the national outrage at the violence in Selma and President Johnon's rhetorical and negotiation/persuasion skills with Congress, the most sweeping civil rights legislation in US history was signed into law.[10] The presence of white-supremacist and anti-immigrant organizations and policies in the US demonstrate an ongoing "loose" understanding of peace and its achievement by many in the US today.[11]

THE INTIMATE RELATIONSHIP OF PEACE WITH WAR

IF YOU WANT PEACE, PREPARE FOR WAR!
The connection of peace with war dates to the 4th and 2nd centuries BC in the writings of the Greek philosopher Plato and the Chinese historian Shi Jin respectively. Each proposed that the way for any nation to enjoy peace was for it to make the necessary military preparations to defend itself. The AD 6th century Roman military general Publius summarized this approach in the formula, *Igitur quī dēsīderat pācem, præparet bellum:* "Therefore let him who desires peace prepare for war." The popular formula of today is the more concise and blunt expression, *si vis pacem, para bellum,* "If you want peace, prepare for war." Be it today military, economic, cyber, whatever type of war conceived, if a nation wants peace and security it must be prepared for war.

The influence of the thinking behind this logic has been profound. The Italian diplomat and philosopher Niccolò di Bernardo dei

Machiavelli (1469 –1527) takes up the theme in his work *Il Principe*, The Prince, published posthumously in 1532. "War," he writes, "should be *the only study of* a prince. He should consider peace only as a breathing-time, which gives him leisure to contrive, and furnishes an ability to execute, military plans...A wise prince then... should never be idle in times of peace but should industriously lay-up stores of which to avail himself in times of adversity so that when Fortune abandons him, he may be prepared to resist her blows."[12] His reference to peace as nothing more than "a breathing time" stands in stark contrast to the lesson that peace cannot simply be the "in-between time" of conflicts learned by the young diplomat Montini while in Poland in 1923.[13] George Washington embraced this philosophy in 1793 when arguing for a standing army and navy at a time when there were deeply held suspicions of a standing military: "There is a rank due to the United States among nations which will be withheld, if not absolutely lost, by the reputation of weakness. If we desire to avoid insult, we must be able to repel it; if we desire to secure peace, one of the most powerful instruments of our rising prosperity, it must be known that *we are at all times ready for war*."[14] [emphasis added]

The Monroe Doctrine of 1823, one might argue, is simply an application of Washington's philosophy presented in a not so veiled threat to the powers of Europe, warning them to stay out of the Americas.[15] In a CBS *60 Minutes* interview the commander of the US Pacific Fleet, Admiral Samuel j. Paparo quoted Publius in the original Latin to summarize the navy's mission today regarding The Peoples' Republic of China: *Si vis pacem, para bellum*. It was, he told the American public, his task to preserve the peace and security for the US by assuring that the navy was prepared for war.[16]

GOING BEYOND BEING PREPARED FOR WAR

There have been variations on this theme. In his 1915 work, *J'accuse*, I Accuse, the German-Jewish pacifist Richard Grelling condemned what he saw as a German policy of what we can describe as *si vis pacem, fac bellum*, "If you want peace, make war." It was this policy and way of thinking about peace that served as the essential cause of the Great War, World War I. The peace Germany wanted can be described as "loose" in that it allowed Germany to make a first strike upon another nation to achieve its own national security goals.

Grelling had reason for this accusation. Even prior to World War I Germany had a history of using war to achieve its security ends. Wanting to bring the southern German states with Prussia into a single, united German nation, Prussian Prime Minister Otto Van Bismark provoked the French Emperor Napolean III into what became known as the Franco-Prussian War in 1870. As has been so often seen throughout history nothing enhances national unity better than war. The gambit worked. A united Germany came to be under the leadership of the Prussian Kaiser Wilhem I, father of the more infamous Wilhem II of World War I. The *Treaty of Frankfurt* ending the war in 1871 gave Germany the added bonus of the French territory of Alsace and large parts of Lorraine. As is the case so often in history, the ending of one war plants the seeds to future conflict. But, for the moment, Bismark achieved his goal of a united, secure Germany: a Germany at peace. Van Bismark wanted unity, security and peace, so he made war.

The moment did not last long. By the early 20th century France was regaining its military strength and was determined to not only reclaim its prestige and lost territory but also to return to what it saw as its rightful place as a power in Europe. France was also engaged in alliance talks with Great Britain, talks that were seen by Germany as a threat to its security from the west. At the same time in the east Czar Nicholas II of Russia was modernizing his nation. With French expertise and financing Russia's single track rail system was being upgraded to double track. This would allow a more efficient transportation network across Russia's vast frontier not only for passengers and commerce, but also allow the rapid mobilization of Russian troops in the event of war.

The "nations-in-the-middle," the central European nations of Germany under Kaiser Wilhem II and its ally the Austro-Hungarian

Empire under the Emperor Franz Joseph I felt threatened by these developments. The assassination of the heir to the Austro-Hungarian throne Archduke Franz Ferdinand and his pregnant wife Sophia on June 28, 1914, by the Serbian nationalist Gavrilo Princip provided the pretext to pursue once again a policy of *si vis pacem, fac bellum* to assure peace and security. Better to have war on Germany's own terms than to wait for the perceived threats from the east and west grow.

In response to the assassination the German military, not the offended Austro-Hungarians, penned an ultimatum to Serbia demanding concessions specifically designed to be rejected. The ultimatum was passed on to Franz Joseph I who, with the assurance of German support should Serbia's ally Russia come to its defense, passed them on to Serbia. Serbia was to accept these demands within 48 hours or face an Austro-Hungarian invasion. In response Russia, which had already mobilized its troops, would most assuredly come to Serbia's defense. This would give Germany an excuse to engage Russia in the east. This would in turn provoke Russia's ally France and provide the pretext for Germany to pro-actively address perceived threats from the west. Serbia was not the point. Serbia was the pretext. Germany instructed the emperor to focus his attention on Russia and to forget about Serbia for the time being, instructions he chose to ignore.[17]

To everyone's surprise Serbia agreed "in principle" to the demands, seeking only clarification of the demand that an investigation of the assassination of the Archduke be conducted in Serbia by the Austro-Hungarian government. The Serbian government had already concluded its own investigation, and might it be found satisfactory. Kaiser Wilhelm II believed war had been averted. The German military command, however, was determined to move forward. After years of the Kaiser's saber-rattling and the modernization of the military Germany's "military industrial complex" was not interested in offering clarifications. The deadline had not been met. The war was on.

To better attack France Germany demanded that Belgium allow its army free passage to invade from then north, allowing the

Germans to go around French defenses at the Maginot Line on Germany's west. Belgium was threatened with invasion if it refused. Germany would go around France's defenses with or without Belgium's cooperation. Belgium's King Albert I, wishing to join the Netherlands in remaining neutral, refused the demand. But this was not a case of "If you want peace, bluff:" Germany invaded. This in turn required Great Britian, a guarantor of Belgian sovereignty, to declare war on Germany. Germany's "If you want peace, make war" policy escalated still further when the Ottman Empire joined the Central Powers in a surprise attack on Russia later that year.[18]

By November 1917 Germany was defeated, an armistice was signed, the fighting ceased. The *Treaty of Versailles* formally ended the war in June 1918. Instead of establishing peace and security, Germany was punished with humiliating demands by the victorious Allies. The Austro-Hungarian and Ottoman Empires were dissolved, something predicted by the heir to the throne whose assassination set off this chain of events. The formula "If you want peace, make war," unlike in 1870, came to disastrous effect. Even so, this formula with its peace/war link has not been fully discredited. The second invasion of Iraq by the United States (2003-2011) was premised on the need to preserve peace and security with a first strike against, as it turned out, nonexistent weapons of mass destruction (WMD). Russia's Vladimir Putin similarly and equally fictitiously used the presence of a "Nazi threat" in Ukraine as an excuse to make a first strike, threatened as it felt it was by Ukraine's pursuit of membership in NATO.[19] Israel has a history of using a "first strike," "If you want peace, make war" approach to peace and security in its response to threats from Iran, and Iran-backed Hezbollah in Lebanon among other terrorist groups.

If making war did not bring security to Germany, neither did victory bring security to the Allies. The humiliation of Germany at the end of the war contributed to an atmosphere that enabled the rise of Adolf Hitler and Nazi ambitions in Europe. Hitler annexed Austria in 1937 and vowed to invade Czechoslovakia on October 1, 1938 to occupy the German-speaking Sudetenland region in a type of, we might say, a *si vis pacem, bellum minaris*, "If you want peace, threaten war." Anxious to avoid a second European conflagration Great Britain's Prime Minister Neville Chamberlin, France's president Edouard Daladier, and Italy's Prime Minister Benito Mussolini met with Hitler in Munich two days before the deadline. In exchange for peace Great Britain and France adopted a policy we might call *si vis pacem, placates*, "If you want peace, appease." The Sudetenland was ceded to Germany with Czechoslovakia having no say in the matter. Chamberlin also secretly signed a non-aggression pact with Hitler. Upon returning from Munich to London he told a cheering crowd that peace had been secured, a "peace for our time." In the end *si vis pacem, placates* proved no more effective in achieving peace and security than *si vis pacem, fac bellum or para bellum*.[20]

Aside from being an ineffective pathway to peace, such formulae have an ironic downside: they increase the risk of war. Linking peace with war has given rise to the arms race and a policy of deterrence, which with nuclear weapons creates yet another formula thought to be acceptable: "If you want peace, assure mutual destruction," *si vis pacem, mutuam perniciem confirmes*. Such preparation makes the security it seeks to assure very fragile with incredibly high risk of miscalculation. We saw this in the Cuban Missile Crisis of 1962. It also legitimizes the possession of nuclear weapons which Paul VI, in contrast to his predecessor Pius XII, opposed. This linkage of peace with war feeds an arms race as each nation seeks to outpace others in destructive technology. Treaties to reduce the number of such arms may have a psychological comforting effect. Still, with all sides limiting the number of missiles only to a level that nevertheless still assures mutual destruction, such comfort such a peace, is deceptive.[21] The risk remains. If there is to be peace a new set of taglines to complete the formula "If you want peace," are needed, taglines grounded in a different, and more "exact meaning of peace."

2
Paul VI and a Theology of Peace

"A nation that continues, year after year,
to spend more on money on military defense
than on programs of social uplift is approaching
spiritual death."
REV. DR. MARTIN LUTHER KING, JR.

INTRODUCTION:
THE ABSENCE OF WAR AND THE PRESENCE OF PEACE

PAUL VI IS A REALIST. HE ADMITS SEVERAL TIMES IN HIS MESSAGES that it seems there will always be individuals and nations intent on using force as a means to their security ends. Russia's "special military operation" in Ukraine is an example of this. We see attempts by subversive groups in different countries to seize power from their government, internal civil conflicts and programs of genocide. With human nature being what it is, some level of military preparation to maintain a *sense* of security, a *kind* of peace, is *seemingly* always, *albeit* tragically, necessary.

Pius XII, though not interested in any direct involvement by the Vatican with an international organization like the UN, stressed the necessity of having such institutions that possessed the authority and ability to negotiate and enforce international agreements in service to achieving world peace. There must be, this pope agreed, some power, some force to reign in terror. The pope has in mind the kind of peace that is the absence of conflict. Looking at his teachings as a whole, explored in some detail in Volume 1, Pius XII and his predecessors put a great deal of confidence in the "right use of force" by a just state or an international entity to maintain peace and security. Paul VI offers an alternative to this notion of the "enforcement" of security as a way to peace, an alternative to any use of force to achieve and preserve peace and security. In his *Peace Messages* can be found alternative taglines to the formula,

"If you want peace" that reflect his "exact idea of peace." These exact ideas are grounded in a common theological understanding of peace obtained from distinct cultural and faith traditions: the Hebrew *Shalom*, the Greek *Eiréné*, and the Latin *Pax*.[22]

The first thing to note in making appeal to this theological approach is that, from Paul VI's perspective, the historical understanding of the relationship between peace and war is inverted. Cold may be the absence of heat, but peace is not the absence of conflict and war. Hence, being prepared for it, let alone making or threatening it cannot possibly lead to genuine or authentic peace. It is war and conflict that reflect absence, the absence of peace. Peace itself is not an absence of something. It is for Paul VI a tangible, recognizable and attainable reality. A *genuine* and *authentic* peace is a tangible presence that is not in any way linked to war and conflict. An excellent example of this way of thinking can be found in the WBUR program "Here and Now," during which host Robin Young interviewed former hostage negotiator Gershon Baskin. They were discussing his thoughts of what Israel needs to do to win the release of the hostages held by Hamas in Gaza. In her interview, Young referred to a plan "to bring about peace." Baskin replied that what she was referring to was simply ending the fighting: "Peace is altogether a different reality."[23]

In his *Messages* Paul VI seeks to articulate for humanity a vison of that tangible, easily identifiable peace not related to war by way of a new papal genre, the *New Year's Peace Messages*. At the UN Paul VI describes himself as speaking first negatively when he proclaims, "Never again war!" *Jamais plus la guerre!* Speaking negatively about war is concise, familiar, easily accessible to his immediate and broader audience. It is far easier to rhetorically call for "Never again war!" than it is to call for "always peace." That however is precisely what Paul VI is doing throughout his 15 years as pope but especially in his *New Year's Peace Messages*. The true focus of his papacy was to speak positively, to speak not of "never again war," but of "always peace." The challenge of this approach is, of course, that we all know what war is. Peace is harder to define if it is to be understood on its own terms.

There is a saying amongst us in Alcoholics Anonymous that a relapse begins long before we take that first drink. In the same way, conflict and war is present long before the first shots are taken because something is missing.[24] For the addict in search of sobriety, a relapse begins with a diminishing appreciation for and engagement in steps necessary for sobriety. For humanity in search of peace, what is missing or being diminished are the tangible elements that define peace. It is those diminishments or absences of peace that he identifies in his *Messages* that ultimately lead to the outbreak of hostilities. As the characteristics of peace offered in his *Peace Messages* are diminished, conflict and war move from cold to cool to warm to hot, with hottest being the use of nuclear weapons. The outbreak of hostilities needs to be seen not simply as the rising of tensions from some international issues of conflict, such as described in Christopher Battman's book, *Why We Fight*,[25] but as the diminishment of the presence of a tangible peace, a reality that can be observed by those paying attention even before there is a noticeable rise in international tensions. If there is to be genuine peace our sights must be set on something higher than the vacuum created in the absence of fighting, especially if this absence reflects attitudes of needing to be prepared for and of fearing war. We must, he challenges us, love peace more than we fear war. We must love a real and tangible peace to treasure it, rather than fear the consequences of its absence. Turning the link between peace and war on its head as Paul VI does, the ancient formula *si vis pacem, para bellum*, "If you want peace, prepare for war," becomes *si vis pacem, creare pacem*: "If you want peace, create peace."

Paul VI will not have us settle for a peace that is nothing more than the "in-between of conflicts" he experienced in Poland during his time there as a diplomat. Peace we can say is like nature which, according to Aristotle, abhors a vacuum. We can say that for Paul VI peace too abhors a vacuum because it is precisely that vacuum that is the root cause of war and conflict. The absence of war is, as

Gershom Baskin told Robin Young cited above, only that. For there to be genuine peace, the vacuum left by the end of war must be filled with the tangible presence of peace itself. Without the presence of peace there is only the absence of fighting, an absence that history teaches again and again will not last.

In an interview with his friend Jean Guitton, Paul VI gives us a clarion call: "We should all always seek peace. Peace for all." Most tellingly he continues, "And though this formidable resolution arose from the searing experience of the war and the fear and terror of seeing it repeated on an apocalyptic scale, today it should be love that supports us. Love of peace rather than fear of war."[26] Peace can only truly be loved when it is a tangible reality. It is not possible to love an absence or a vacuum, impossible to love an "in-between" of any kind. True peace, his theological background informs him, is the fruit "of a concrete, continuous and unanimous effort for the construction of a local and universal community founded on human solidarity in the search for a common, universal good.[27] Time now to take a close look at the faith traditions upon which so much of the teachings of Paul VI on peace are built.

PEACE FROM THE HEBREWS: SHALOM

The Hebrew term *shalom* is most often understood as a common expression of peace in a greeting. Much more is being said. The root of *shalom* is *shalam*. One of the first uses of shalam in the Torah is found in Exodus 21 & 22, where it is used 14 times. The narrative is that of Moses giving instructions to the people about how to address a situation in which someone causes a material loss to another. This may be by damaging or destroying property or livestock, as well as in cases of theft. As a result of damage or harm done the victim is said to be now lacking in something. The victim is not simply lacking livestock, but to be lacking in some way as a person: the victim is no longer complete or whole. Moses teaches that the one responsible for causing this state of "incompleteness" has an obligation to return the victim to a state of *shalam*: a state of completeness, a state of wholeness.

Shalam is a matter of making restitution for the harm done understood in its most literal sense. Restitution is not simply restoring or replacing what was damaged or lost to somehow "make up" for what was done, such as seen in the demands made by the victors for reparations from the defeated. Taken literally from its Latin root, *re – statuere*, restitution means to "re-establish" a person or society to his/her/their full humanity. Understood in this way restitution cannot be pursued without reconciliation. Understood from the Latin root, *reconciliare*, reconciliation has as its meaning to "re-establish friendly relations." The Hebrew *shalam* and by extension *shalom*, as with the English restitution and reconciliation seen in the pope's 1970 and 1975 *Messages*, refer not to the re-establishment of the material dimension of the loss, but of human dimension. There is no "eye for an eye" being demanded (Exodus 21,23-27), or appeal to "exact retaliation" (*lex talionis*), but instead a returning of the one harmed to a human completeness that has been lost. We see this understanding of the Hebrew *shalom* in the narrative of Joseph and his brothers in Genesis, 43.

Joseph is the youngest and favorite son of his father Jacob; his mother having been Jacob's favorite wife. His brothers are envious and plot to kill him, but instead sell him into enslavement in Egypt. Because he possesses the gift of interpreting dreams Joseph is able to help Egypt avoid famine during a prolonged drought. He is rewarded by Pharo with a position of authority. It is during this famine that Joseph's' brothers go to Egypt seeking relief, finding themselves unknowingly pleading before their long-forgotten younger brother. In verses 27-28 Joseph inquiries about his father's health. The conversation repeatedly uses the Hebrew *shalom*: "Then he asked them about their *well-being*, and said, 'Is your father *well*, the old man of whom you spoke? Is he still alive?' And they answered, 'Your servant our father is in *good health*; he is still alive.'"[28] *Shalom*, as a greeting or a statement of fact, expresses an understanding of peace as a tangible presence, a presence of human, personal wholeness and well-being. *Shalom* is a state of peace that cannot be imposed or achieved by force, nor does it lend itself to the type of "loose" interpretation described by Parchami in Chapter 1.

PEACE FROM THE GREEKS: EIRÉNÉ

The notion of peace in the use of the Greek *Eiréné* is similar to that of *shalom*, perhaps surprisingly so, but with an important exception. While the Hebrew *shalom* is a "concept" of peace that embraces the human dimension of element of wholeness, for the ancient Greeks peace is "personified." Far from peace being a concept, peace is personified as a "goddess," and the mythological Greek goddess of peace is *Eiréné*. Because peace is personified as a goddess, it is possible to gain insight into the meaning of genuine peace by looking at her personal features as they are presented in art and in Greek temples. The goddess *Eiréné* is presented to us as a beautiful, we can even say voluptuous women. Most often she is holding a cornucopia overflowing with fruits and vegetables, flowers and nuts.[29] Similarly, she is often shown holding the infant Plutus, the mythological Greek god of wealth. The significance of his presence with *Eiréné* is further emphasized in that *Plutus* is the son of *Demeter*, the goddess of grain, agriculture, and the harvest. It *Demeter's* role as a goddess to watch over and protect the fertility of the earth and the peoples' crops.

It should not be missed that while the Hebrew *shalom* entails the meaning of interpersonal relationships of friendship and wholeness, amongst the Greek mythological gods there is also seen the importance of relationships. One might say that for the ancient Greeks, peace is a "family affair." As with *shalom*, although perhaps more easily recognizable with *Eiréné* and her divine companions, the reality of peace cannot be simplified as the absence of conflict. Peace is a presence, the presence of a tangible and life-giving abundance. Such a peace cannot be imposed, nor does it lend itself to a "loose" interpretation and implementation. Rather, it should be sought, embraced and celebrated. Paul VI will tell us in his *Messages* that peace needs to be created, made, even invented.

PEACE FROM THE LATINS: PAX

As with the Greek *Eiréné*, peace is once again personified as a goddess, the Roman mythological goddess *Pax*. It must though first be noted that, in a somewhat odd and unexpected twist, the English word "peace" does not come, as generally supposed, from the Latin *Pax*. Our English term is derived from the Anglo-Norman term *pas*. This is significant. As with shalom, pas denotes a concept of peace, but a very different one indeed! The peace of which *pas* speaks is closer to the contemporary and operative understanding of peace as the absence of conflict. We are it seems linguistically inclined to think of peace in this simplistic way. The peace denoted by *pas* entails none of the dimensions or elements of human wholeness as does *shalom*, or any of the richness of *Eiréné* nor, as about to be explored, *Pax*.

Personified as a Roman goddess we are again able to draw insights into the genuine meaning of peace by noticing her parentage and her interpersonal relationships with other mythological figures. *Pax* is the daughter of the Roman god <u>Jupiter</u> and *Justitia*, the goddess of <u>justice</u>. *Jupiter*, like *Zeus* in Greek mythology, is the supreme god and king of a pantheon of gods. *Jupiter* was the god of the heavens and thunder and, importantly in this context, the god of "law and order." He is often portrayed with a lightning bolt in his hand symbolizing his power. *Justitia* is portrayed blindfolded and holding scales in a balance. The expression often heard in American jurisprudence "justice is blind" or "blind justice" is an allusion to the justice *Justitia* represents. We can say perhaps that *Pax's* parentage is that of the strong arm to assure security that is tempered with fairness and the blind protection of equality. One might here think of James 2, 13: "For judgement is merciless to one who has not shown mercy; mercy triumphs over judgement."[30]

As with *Eiréné*, the manner in which *Pax* is expressed in Roman art and temple worship gives us insight into the richness of peace beyond the ending of hostilities. The first images of *Pax* on Roman coins show her surrounded by farm animals. In later art she is commonly depicted holding out <u>olive</u> branches as a peace offering.

The association of the olive branch with a mythical goddess may be original to the Romans, but the association of the olive branch with peace dates to 5th century BC Greece. Because of the similarities and even identification between the gods of Greek and Roman mythology [31] it is easy to see why the Romans would borrow the olive branch as a symbol of peace from the Greeks, for whom it represented abundance and drove away evil spirits, to identify their own goddess of peace. *Pax* is similarly portrayed with an overflowing cornucopia as well as at times with stalks of corn. She is also often associated with the new life associated with spring.

FINAL THOUGHTS

The title of Part One asks a Shakespearian question: "To Link or not to link" war with peace. As seen in Chapter 1 the dominant response throughout history and until now is: "Yes, there is a link, a connection." The link must be made because, it is held, peace is the absence of any threat to security, of conflict and war. "If we want peace" as the adage goes, we must accept some connection with war and conflict. The most common link between peace and war is to be prepared for war. There is, as Machiavelli wrote, no other responsibility of the prince than to use the time between conflicts to plan and be prepared for the next. There are examples in the past and recently of linking peace with making war, be it to unite and strengthen a nation's resolve, or to make a "first strike" before an enemy can launch an attack. Some leaders have threatened war to achieve security. Such threats are historically not idle threats. At times it has been hoped that appeasing an enemy will secure peace by eliminating, or at least diminishing or delaying an attack.

None of these approaches has achieved the "absence of war" definition of peace. On the contrary, the logic that the best way to achieve peace is in some way linked to war has only made a state of an absence of war more precarious as it has engendered an arms race that devotes resources disproportionately towards a "military industrial complex" and away from programs that lift people up to live full, happy, meaningful lives in a safe and secure environment.[32]

As hostage negotiator Gershon Baskin told Robin Young in an interview cited above, ending war is not achieving peace. [33] Similarly, neither preventing war nor preventing the escalation of an ongoing conflict has any link to peace. Neither *shalom*, *Eiréné* nor *Pax* have any link to war, just as the Anglo-Norman pas has no link to peace.

Far from being an absence, peace is a tangible, recognizable and achievable presence. Peace is the presence of human wholeness, of abundance and prosperity, of security tempered by a justice not blind to the socio-economic inequalities in the world, inequalities that must be addressed if there is to be peace. This multi-national vision is clearly articulated in his 1967 encyclical *Populorum progressio* in which he defines "development" as the new name for peace. Nor, as will be seen in his *Messages*, is justice blind to the discriminations that plague any society in any nation, in any country. The concept of *shalom* and the insights drawn from the personification of the Greek and Roman mythological goddesses of peace provide a theological foundation for Paul VI's *Peace Messages* as he presents his "exact idea of peace," and the pathway to its genuine, tangible, measurable presence in the world. It is to that exact idea of peace and the pathways to it we now turn in Part Two.

PART TWO

———

"IF YOU WANT PEACE... "
THE INSIGHTS OF PAUL VI

3
New Year's Messages 1968 - 1973

"First of all, you must love peace."
PAUL VI, HOMILY YANKEE STADIUM, 1965

1968 – "ANNOUNCING AN ANNUAL DAY OF PEACE"

BACKGROUND 1967

Vietnam saw an escalation of conflict of both on the ground and from the air with the expansion *Operation Thunder*, the bombing campaign begun by President Johnson in March of 1965. As the war was expanding Secretary of Defense Robert McNamara commissioned a task force to study the history of US political and military involvement in Vietnam from 1945 to 1967. The report, with the official title, "Report of the office of the Secretary of Defense Vietnam Task Force," later became known simply as the "Pentagon Papers." One of the analysts on the task force was a man by the name of Daniel Elberg, about whom we will learn more in the historical brief to the 1977 *Message*. One immediate result of the Report was the November 1 "top-secret" memorandum McNamara sent to Johnson recommending a reduction of military operations. He would later describe in a memoir he said he never intended to write, "We of the Kennedy and Johnson administrations who participated in the decisions on Vietnam acted according to what we thought were the principles and traditions of this nation...were wrong, terribly wrong. We owe it to future generations to explain why."[34] It was just a month later, just days before Christmas, that the president made his surprise visit to the Vatican to "set the pope straight" on Vietnam.[35]

MESSAGE 1968: - THE DAY OF PEACE

There are two audiences in Paul VI's inaugural Message. He first speaks, as he does in all his writings following the example of his immediate predecessor John XXIII, to "all men of goodwill." He is calling on all peoples to celebrate a Day of Peace "throughout the world on the first day of this and every year." These annual celebrations should be seen as "a hope and as a promise that Peace, with its just and beneficent equilibrium, may dominate the development of events to come." His introduction of the phrase "just and beneficent equilibrium" here is significant as he will develop the concept of a balancing of interests amongst nations to achieve an equilibrium as a counterpoint to the notion that deterrence and a balance of arms can lead to peace.

He is confident that all humanity will respond positively to this invitation, writing that such a day "captures the aspirations of peoples...which make Peace their ideal." He speaks in 1968 as he does so often of and to the youth of the world, "whose perspicacity regarding the new paths of civilization, dutifully oriented toward its peaceful developments, is more lively." He is in these comments no doubt reminiscing of his days as a chaplain as a newly ordained priest. This "day of peace" is not intended for Catholics alone to observe, although he will explicitly challenge the faithful to be engage in working for peace in his 1975 Message, as he did in his Marian encyclicals in 1965 and 1967. It is his sincere hope that beginning each year with a day to celebrate peace will "have the adherence of all the true friends of Peace." The Church "simply wishes to launch the idea" in the hope that it may not only receive the widest acceptance, but that such an idea might "give to the history of the world a more happy, ordered and civilized development."

An important characteristic of a Day of Peace, one to which he will return in later years, is the defense of peace in the face of the many dangers that threaten it. He mentions the danger of selfishness among nations and of the choice of violence chosen by some who live under political oppression or economic deprivation. He speaks as well of those weapons for which nations make an enormous financial investment, "which hinder the development of so many other peoples." He has already touched on this issue the previous year in his encyclical *Populorum Progressio*, "On the Progress of Peoples." He speaks now of a danger that remains in our own time, a damager which "is today tremendously increased," as nations have recourse to "frightful weapons of extermination." He notes, as he did in his address in India in 1964 and repeatedly expressed throughout his papacy, that the cost of such weapons and the arms race "is reason for painful reflection in the presence of the grave needs which hinder the development of so many other peoples."

Perhaps the most dangerous threat to peace he suggests is the belief by many "that international controversies cannot be resolved by the way of reason, that is, by negotiations founded on law, justice, and equity," but only by appeal to deterrence or force. "Negotiation" is perhaps not the best English term to capture Paul VI's thinking. He is very much a man and pope of dialogue, from the Greek *dialogos* meaning "conversation." As noted in Chapter 1 of Volume 1 Paul VI was the first pope to use the term in an official Church document. We find its first use, where it is then repeated thirteen times, in his first encyclical *Ecclesia Suam*, "His [Christ's] Church," in 1964. Paul VI will never abandon the conviction that "dialogue" is the pathway to that "equilibrium" that is peace. These dangers bring him to issue a warning in this inaugural address: "Peace cannot be based on a false rhetoric of words which are welcomed because they answer to the deep, genuine aspirations of humanity, but which can also serve, and unfortunately have sometimes served, to hide the lack of true spirit and of real intentions for peace if not indeed to mask sentiments and actions of oppression and party interests."

"False rhetoric" cannot bring about peace, "even if, perchance, oppression is able to create the external appearance of order and legality." This deceptively attractive state of security can only result, he writes somewhat prophetically, in "an unceasing and insuppressible growth of revolt and war." It is not possible to speak of peace without "a recognition or respect for its solid foundations of sincerity, justice and love in the relations between states." This is true not merely *among* but also *within* nations, "between citizens and their governments in a celebration of civic, cultural, moral and religious freedom."[36] It is, then, "in the sincere recognition of the rights of the human person and of the independence of the individual nations, that We invite men of wisdom and strength to dedicate this Day." The annual New Year's Peace Messages inaugurated January 1, 1968, are Paul VI's opportunity to present new pathways to peace.

It does need to be noted that in this inaugural *Message* Paul VI betrays a prejudice towards "pacifism" seen in his writings discussed in Volume 1. He writes, "It is to be hoped that the exaltation of the ideal of Peace may not favour the cowardice of those who fear it may be their duty to give their life for the service of their own country and of their own brothers...and who seek only a flight from their responsibility. Peace is not pacifism." As this prejudice and criticism of it are explored in Chapter 3 of that volume, I will simply make note of it here and not explore it in these commentaries.

Paul VI's second audience is the Church itself. As he is creating a new genre of papal teaching he needs to establish a foundation and justification. He reminds the faithful that it is his duty, as universal pastor, to be a prophetic voice for peace. He writes, "Peace is part and parcel of the Christian religion, since for a Christian to proclaim peace is the same as to announce Jesus Christ: 'He is our peace.'" (Eph. ii. 14) The Good News he proclaims is a "Gospel of peace." (Eph. vi. 15) Quoting John XXIII's *Pacem in terris*, he calls on Catholics to join with him to "arouse in the men of our time and of future generations a sense of Peace founded upon truth, justice, freedom and love."

He also wants to affirm for the Catholic audience that the Celebration of a *Day of Peace* does not change the liturgical calendar which reserves New Year's Day as the "Solemnity of Mary, Mother of God," and "The Octave Day of the Nativity of the Lord."[37] Adding a focus on peace, he writes, complements the Solemnity for "those holy and loving religious remembrances [of Mary] must shed their light of goodness, wisdom and hope upon the prayer for, the meditation upon, and the fostering of the great and yearned-for gift of Peace, of which the world has so much need." Aside from the logic of choosing the first day of the year as a day of peace, Paul VI offers a theological and liturgical reason for choosing January first.

And finally, prayer, Paul VI reminds us, is humanity's singular "weapon" for Peace. He will return in his 1976 *Message* to the rather ironic reference to there being "weapons" for peace. His 1978 Message will bring these writings to a close calling for prayer and the "contemplation" of peace. For now, we note with him that, with all its "marvelous energies," prayer is an opportunity "to question ourselves interiorly and sincerely concerning the roots of rancor and violence that may lurk deep in our hearts." Doing so can bring about the spiritual, social, psychological and political renewal the world needs to find peace.

1969 – THE PROMOTION OF HUMAN RIGHTS AS THE WAY TO PEACE

BACKGROUND 1968
IN VIETNAM, January 31,1968, saw the beginning of the North Vietnamese *Tet Offensive* during which some 85,000 troops from the North simultaneously attacked major South Vietnamese cities, military installations, and scores of smaller towns and villages. This would be followed by Tet *1969* in February the following year. In both assaults the US and South Vietnamese prevailed, but at a great price. With the war's mounting casualties more Americans, including many of those Catholics who had been supportive of the war at its beginning, began to think differently. Like his predecessor at the Defense Department, the new Secretary Clark Clifford added his voice to the call to scale down US involvement.[38] Negotiations between the US and North Vietnam began in 1968, negotiations in which Paul VI played a major role in initiating, at the behest of President Johnson described in some detail in Chapter 6 of Volume 1.

MESSAGE 1969: - THE PROMOTION OF HUMAN RIGHTS

Paul VI used his inaugural *Message* to do just that: inaugurate, explain, invite. With this as his singular focus, he passed on noting 1968 as the 20th anniversary of the *United Nations Declaration of Human Rights*. I make note of this because as will be seen Paul VI is as it were "laser focused" in his speeches and writings.[39] This is clearly seen in his singular focus on peace during his 1965 visit to New York. Even the time and place of his meeting with President Johnson was so arranged as to not distract from his singular mission: his call for "never again war!" To combine both his inaugural focus with a celebration of the *Declaration* for the sake of the calendar would diminish both. First, he initiates and focuses exclusively on his getting his *New Year's Messaging* "off the ground." Human Rights enjoys his full attention in 1969: "This year a special circumstance recommends Our proposal to all: there has been celebrated the twenty-fifth [sic – (twentieth)] anniversary of the *Declaration of Human Rights*."[40]

Soon after the founding of the UN in San Francisco in 1945 President Harry Truman asked Eleanor Roosevelt to lead the US effort to encourage the UN to adopt a *Universal Declaration of Human Rights*. Such a declaration would enshrine as "inalienable" and "inviolable" those rights that belong to and are guaranteed for all of humanity. The *Declaration* was adopted December 10, 1948, at the 10th Session of the General Assembly at the Palais de Chaillot, Paris, France. In this 1969 *Message* Paul VI speaks of the essential and reciprocal relationship peace and human rights enjoy. They are each other's cause and effect. Human Rights are "the most fundamental of rights to be enjoyed by all peoples in all nations." An emphatic statement in his Message is worth quoting at length: "When Peace loses its equilibrium and efficiency, Human Rights become precarious and are compromised. There is no peace...Moreover, where Human Rights are not respected, defended, or promoted, where violence and fraud is done to man's inalienable freedoms, where his personality is ignored or degraded, where discrimination, slavery or intolerance prevail, there true Peace cannot be."

He observes that "Peace favors Human Rights, and Human Rights favor peace." As he called "development" the new word for peace two years earlier in his 1967 encyclical *Populorum Progressio*, he might have, and implicitly does, define Human Rights as the new word for peace. The inverse might also be said as true: peace is another word for Human Rights."

He calls out to the youth of the world, calling on them to accept his invitation to embrace and work for peace by promoting Human Rights. He expresses the sentiment that their spirits are "exasperated," and that there is "a great agitation of their irritated souls" stemming from a continuing need to correct the abuses of Human Rights throughout the world. However great the abuses and however irritated their souls Paul VI nevertheless calls on everyone of goodwill, "all those responsible for the development of history today and tomorrow" to hold to the hope that with the help of the youth the world can, as he challenged the UN, "Go forward!" A quote from earlier in the text captures this call poetically: "the first sun of the new year must shed upon the earth the light of Peace."

There must be he insists an "inexhaustible optimism" informing our pursuit of peace, an optimism rooted in the Peace of Christ: "Christ's Peace infuses the unconquerable energy of those rights derived from the deepest reasons of human nature and from man's transcendental destiny." There must be, reflecting his conviction of nonviolence in the pursuit of Human Rights, "not a fear of might, and resistance." The work of Human Rights in the name of the Peace of Christ, "understands pain and human needs, which finds love and gifts for the little, the poor, the weak the disinherited, the suffering." The Peace of Christ is "more than any other humanitarian formula, solicitous of Human Rights." Paul VI's own solicitousness of Human Rights earned him recognition as an International Innovator of Human Rights."[41] He is the only pope to date to have been given this honor. Among his "innovations" of the papacy's engagement in world affairs was his public embracing and supporting of the nonviolent pursuit of civil and labor rights led in the US by such leaders as Rev. Martin Luther King, Jr., and Ceasar Chavez, both of whom he received and with whom he was photographed at the Vatican.[42] We also see "innovations" in his naming the first Black bishop in the US since 1875.[43] On September 29, 1965, Harold Robert Perry, SVD, was named by Paul VI to be auxiliary bishop of the Archdiocese of New Orleans.[44] Perry would not be the bishop of color he would name. As it happened, the very last American bishop he named before his passing in 1978 was a man of color. Paul VI can also be said to be "innovative" in his naming of White bishops supportive of civil and labor rights and, as he did with Perry, appointing them to dioceses where they would have the greatest impact.[45]

If Paul VI were to explicitly offer a new tagline for the formula "If you want peace...," his 1969 Message clearly points to the necessity of promoting human rights: "If you want peace, promote human rights." Human Rights are a tangible, recognizable, achievable presence, that is the presence of peace.

1970 – "TO BE RECONCILED WITH EACH OTHER"

BACKGROUND 1969
FOR VIETNAM there was a change of administration and with it a change in US strategy. Richard Nixon was now president, having defeated former Vice President Hubert Humphrey in the 1968 election. Nixon had campaigned on the promise he would end the war in Vietnam while preserving America's honor. He would ultimately adopt Benedict XV's call to peace without victory per se. There is an implicit admission that the war was, as more and more people and especially Catholics came to believe, unwinnable. Catholics were moving away from following the support for the war of such Catholic leaders as New York's Cardinal Archbishop Francis Spellman, who passed away in December of 1967, and closer to the opposition of their pope.[46] Some form of peace that allowed the US to save face was the new military and political goal.

Rejecting calls for an immediate withdrawal of troops Nixon set as his foreign policy goal an "honorable peace" that left South Vietnam with a stable, democratic Republic capable of defending itself after the US withdrew. Achieving peace in Southeast Asia now shifted to ending US engagement in the current conflict with preparations to prevent another. We might suggest Nixon is embracing the ancient formula with a more geographical tagline, "If you want peace in Vietnam, prepare for war in Vietnam."

To get the US out of Vietnam and try to mollify at least some in the anti-war movement Nixon and his Secretary of Defense Melvin Laird introduced a strategy they called the *Vietnamization* of the war: a gradual withdrawal of US forces combined with expanded efforts to train and equip South Vietnam military. This strategy was presented to the nation in a televised speech on November 3, 1969. To help build public support for his *Vietnamization* strategy, it can be said he somewhat threw his predecessor Lyndon Johnson "under the bus." To the American public he announced, "The defense of freedom is everybody's business, not just America's business. And it is particularly the responsibility of the people whose freedom is threatened...In the previous administration, we *Americanized* the war in Vietnam. In this administration, we are *Vietnamizing* the search for peace."[47] The *Vietnamization* of the war did not affect in any way the escalating US bombing in Vietnam, nor its later expansion to neighboring neutral countries. Nor did it lessen Paul VI's critiques.

Meanwhile the former marine and military analyst Daniel Elsberg mentioned previously made a photocopy of the 1967 "Top-Secret-Sensitive" report he had helped prepare for then Defense Secretary McNamara. Upon seeing the true extent of US involvement in Vietnam, as well as the political and strategic errors of which McNamara later wrote, Elsberg began his conversion from military analyst to anti-war activist. In an effort to try to bring the conflict to an end he published these documents as *The Pentagon Papers* in 1971 in the *New York Times and The Washington Post*. He was later charged with espionage, charges later dismissed.

MESSAGE: - 1970 "TO BE RECONCILED WITH EACH OTHER"

Paul VI begins with a creative salutation, a salutation that concludes with a haunting question: CITIZENS OF THE WORLD! *As you salute the dawn of this new year nineteen hundred and seventy, take thought for a moment: Whither is mankind's path leading?*

Paul VI begins by affirming that through study, science, work and the tools of technology, humanity "seeks to live a better and fuller life." Not surprisingly given his worldview, he asserts that aspirations for a better life cannot be realized for any one people or nation unless it is realized by all peoples of all nations. Humanity must "extend the benefits of progress to all peoples," at the same time striving for "that unity, justice, balance and perfection, which we call Peace." This definition of peace, to which he alludes throughout all his *Messages*, speaks to his concept of peace as a matter of balance, an equilibrium," from the Latin *aequilibrium* meaning "an even balance," of competing national interests he referenced in his inaugural *Message* two years previous. Far from being a static and ordered security, peace is a constantly evolving dynamic, an "equilibrium of national and individual interests achieved through dialogue, through conversation." He does not hesitate to nudge the Catholic tradition's understanding of peace as relying on a more state managed order to this more dynamic understanding he will continue to develop through these annual *Messages*.

He notes, as have we, that peace has been primarily understood as the absence of chaos and conflict, the absence of disorder. As he has mentioned previously, an exaggeration of the need to preserve order easily lends itself too easily to the imposition of a peaceful order, a loose understanding of peace as described in Chapter 1 above that can and has led to abuses of human rights. The imposition of order gives, he asserts once again, the deceptive "pretense" of peace. For Paul VI peace is better understood as establishing a dynamic balancing of interests and ideologies, an insight drawn from his love of dialogue. To speak of order as peace is to too easily think of a static state that can be readily identified and enforced. He calls this an "immobile tranquility" that is "paralyzing and selfish." He understands in a new way, as previously described, St Augustine's concept of peace as a "tranquility of order." Augustine has in mind the pope insists not a static reality but a dynamic balancing of different, at times complementary, at times competing and at times conflicting interests. Peace is, as the popular expression suggests, always "a work in progress." In citing the same texts of Augustine used in the past to support a static understanding of peace as order in support of his understanding of peace, he is moving well beyond the traditional stance of the Catholic tradition grounded in the tradition's historical deference to legitimate authority in maintaining that order. Again referring to Augustine, Paul VI holds that to be a "truly human" order or stability, it must be recognized as a reality that is always able to be improved, to be "perfectible." Peace "is unceasingly brought to being and developed...it lies in a progressive motion." Peace is a moment of equilibrium that can be enjoyed when we have a just and loving balance of mutual, similar, competing and even conflicting interests found not through negotiation in which each side seeks to gain as much as possible and give up as little as necessary to come to agreement, but through conversation through which each side "chooses" to become friend, the theme of his 1971 *Message*.

Referring to his readers as "friends" he explains, "We do not put before you a state of repressive, selfish inertia." Here he offers one of, I believe, his more profound insights: "Peace is not enjoyed: it is created." We "create peace" in our dialogues, our seeking of an equilibrium of interests among peoples. He observes, and no one would argue, "that we have not yet reached the fullness of that peace we are called to create, that peace to which each and every one of us must aspire." Peace remains for us always that "work in progress," a most necessary ongoing work in progress.

An essential element of creating peace is reconciliation, the principal theme of this *Message*. We might rephrase into the positive his call at the UN for "never again once against the other" to "always one reconciled with the other." Our English term "reconciliation" comes from the Latin *reconsiliare*, meaning "to be bring together," or "to make friendly again." Paul VI's 1970 *Message* is that peace is achieved by creating and re-creating friendships, by the coming together of others in dialogue between and amongst friends and belligerents, allies and adversaries alike. It is when opposing nations, interests, and ideologies are reconciled in a dynamic balancing, an equilibrium, that we create true and genuine peace. Reconciliation is the path to "that unity, justice, balance and perfection" which is peace. The necessity of reconciliation in achieving peace is a theme reminiscent of the 1917 Peace Note of his predecessor Benedict XV during World War I. Had the "one against the other" of World War I been followed by a "one reconciled with the other" in negotiating the treaty ending the war, as advocated by the pope, the course of history would most certainly have been different.

Reconciliation is for Paul VI absolutely necessary to secure genuine peace and prevent future conflict. Ending or pausing conflict, be it a truce, cease-fire or armistice must be followed not solely by a negotiated settlement, but by a reconciliation between the belligerent parties. It is not enough to simply stop fighting. In language reminiscent of Benedict XV Paul VI rightly asks, "If Peace is without clemency, how can it be called Peace? If Peace is imbued with the spirit of revenge," no doubt thinking of the unnecessary bombing by the allies of historical, cultural and spiritual sites in Europe towards the end of World War II examined in Chapter 7 of Volume 1, "how can it be true Peace?" All sides need to make "an appeal to *that superior justice, which is pardon*." [emphasis added] We are called beyond a narrow notion of justice to the idea that there is yet a superior justice, that of reconciliation. Paul VI offers to us the notion of thinking about justice as pardon. This superior justice, this pardoning, "cancels out insoluble questions of prestige, and makes friendship possible once again." Paul VI may be thinking of St Peter's letter in which he reminds the early Christians, and us today, that "love covers a multitude of sins." (1 Peter 4,8)

The pope readily admits that preaching the Gospel of pardon and reconciliation "seems absurd to human politics." It seems illogical, incongruous, even foolish. This is because in our socio-political environment, "justice does not often permit forgiveness." Especially for Christians however, he believes that a Gospel of reconciliation as a pathway to peace "is not absurd. Difficult, yes, but not absurd." He accepts that reconciliation often poses a difficult challenge, "But" he poetically asks, "is it not a magnificent one?"[48] If Paul VI were to offer in 1970 a new formula for peace it would most certainly be, "If you want peace, be reconciled with each other." We might even take the liberty of offering an entirely new formula: "If you want to create peace, be reconciled."

1971 – "EVERY MAN IS MY BROTHER"

BACKGROUND 1970
IN VIETNAM US troop withdrawal and *Vietnamization* continued even as there was no progress in the Paris Talks. Given the role Paul VI played in getting these talks started their continued futility was surely an ongoing disappointment for him. The speed with which Hanoi had responded to the pope's invitation at the behest of Johnson in 1968 certainly must have inspired hope that negotiations would move along, if not quickly at least progressively. His disappointment was perhaps especially so as Nixon broadened the air and ground war into Cambodia and Laos.

The North Vietnamese supported the Khmer Rouge in the Cambodian civil war. US and South Vietnamese forces invaded southeast Cambodia in April 1970. This "If you want peace, make war," first-strike invasion was "justified" it was said as part of the *Vietnamization* of the war effort. The invasion was meant to prevent the North Vietnamese and Viet Cong troops from using Cambodia's border with South Vietnam as a safe staging platform from which to attack the South, as was the case previously in Laos. US troops remained in Cambodia until the end of July.

The expansion of the war was greeted with an expansion of the anti-war movement in the US, a movement that was at times fatal for the protesters. On May 4, four students were killed and nine wounded at Kent State University when the Ohio National Guard opened fire on protesters. Just 11 days later, May 15, Mississippi State Police opened fire on a group of student protestors at Jackson

State University killing 2 and wounding 12. These and similar events further enflamed anti-war sentiments in Congress. In response to Nixon's expanding of the war effort Congress passed the Cooper-Church Amendment meant to prevent the reintroduction of US troops into Cambodia as well as to prohibit the future introduction of US troops to any other Southeast Asia country.[49] The legislation did not prohibit US air support of South Vietnamese troops in their continued campaign in Cambodia, nor did it prohibit continued military aid going to the Cambodian government to fight the Khmer Rouge. Even with this support the Cambodian government continued to lose control of vast areas of the country to the Khmer Rouge. The legitimate government was finally defeated in April 1975. The Khmer Rouge's brutal rule would last to 1979.

MESSAGE 1971: – "EVERY MAN IS MY BROTHER!"

Again, a creative salutation:

MEN OF 1971!
On the timepiece of the world's history
the hand of time,
of our time,
points to the beginning of a new year this one
which We wish to inaugurate,
as We have inaugurated previous years,
with Our affectionate greeting,
with Our message of Peace:
Peace to you, Peace to the world.

The prior year, 1970, marked the 25th anniversary of the end of the Second World War with the formal surrender of Japan on September 2, 1945. The war in Europe had ended with Germany's surrender on May 8. Paul VI marks this anniversary in his 1971 *Message* noting that in 1945 the entire world cried out: "Enough! Enough of...everything that gave rise to the human butchery and the appalling devastation." The action of the Allies after the war would suggest that they agreed there had been indeed "Enough." It is true that the victors of the war did take a page out of the approach of the victors of World War I. Roosevelt, Stalin and Churchill took it upon themselves at the Yalta Conference February 4-11, 1945, to decide amongst themselves the future shape of Europe without any input from any of the European nations. Still, far from seeking retribution and reparations, Europe as a whole was able to heal thanks to US backed and funded programs such as the Marshall Plan, named for then Secretary of State George Marshall in 1947.[50] Similarly, rather than blaming the German population as a whole for Hitler's war and the war crimes committed as in the Treaty of Versailles ending World War I, individuals were held responsible and faced the Nuremburg Trials of 1945-1946.

In this more reconciliatory approach Paul VI sees an example of reconciliation that might inspire the hope "that a new era was about to open, the era of universal peace." There seemed to be an acceptance that radical changes in international relations were necessary to avoid future conflicts. Among those are what he referred to as "wonderful moral and social innovations." There was talk of justice, the recognition of human rights, of lifting the poor and weak of the world. It seemed to Paul VI that the world had begun to think in terms of an orderly co-existence and organized collaboration. He makes specific reference to the Marshall Plan, the victors coming to the aid of rather than seeking retribution from the vanquished. He speaks with optimism of the possibility of peace being "a normal and fundamental condition of life in the world." Who but Paul VI would dare to speak of peace as a "normal" condition of everyday life?

Now however, twenty-five years after this "material and idyllic progress" he admits, "that, here and there, wars still rage. We see a continuation of, and in some places an increase in, social, racial and religious discrimination. "The demons of yesterday," he laments, "rise up again." He observes that, "Once again people feel a tremor of fear lest some catastrophic imprudence might lead to incredible and uncontrollable holocausts." Instead of peace being found in the balance of interests, it became "no more than a balance of mighty forces and of terrifying armaments." Paul VI painted a bleak portrait of the world and prospects for peace in 1971. This particular paragraph is possibly the most pessimistic assessment of the world he gives in any of his annual *Messages*. It stands out in such stark contrast from the optimism of the solidarity that initially emerged at the end of the war.

While his primary focus on peace in these *Messages* has been up to now from an international perspective, it was perhaps already noticed from the quotes above that he speaks also in 1971 of the demons arising *within* nations. Among other challenges he mentions class hatred and class warfare. Knowing of his concern for Africa and his attempt to intervene in the Nigerian Civil War during his trip to Uganda in 1969, we can think here that he might point also to the tribal warfare that has and continues to plague parts of Africa, a continent towards which he had a particular affection. In addition to his concerns of social, racial, and religious discrimination, he points to a return of the "supremacy of economic interests" leading to exploitation of the poor. An example is the violations of Child Labor Laws being disclosed today in the US where it happens that children, whose wages are below that of an adult, work more or later hours and in more hazardous jobs than allowed by law.[51] This pessimistic assessment ends with his identifying these developments as seemingly "incurable wounds" that threaten to spread and worsen. He asks the haunting questions of the *Messages* salutation above: "What is happening? Where are we going? What has gone wrong?"

But then, as if out of nowhere, comes that familiar optimism. "Happily," he says, it is possible to speak of a "progressive peace." To continue this progress we must make an "identity of choice." We must choose, he writes, to become friends with one another. Paul VI calls us to choose as our identity that of being "friend." If we want peace, he writes with tremendous insight into human relations,

"We must recognize the necessity of building [friendships] upon foundations more substantial than the nonexistence of relations,(relations among men are inevitable; they grow and become necessary), or the existence of relations of self-interest, (these are precarious and often deceptive), or the web of purely cultural or fortuitous relations, (these can be double-edged, for peace or for combat)."

In support of the importance of friendship for peace he cites the 13th century philosopher St Thomas Aquinas: "Peace is love, true love, human love." He might have once again made appeal to St Augustine who wrote so beautifully of friendship in his *Confessions*: "The friendship which draws human beings together in a tender bond is sweet to us because out of many minds it forges a unity." In the name of peace, we are called to make the existential choice to be a friend to one another in society. We can do this, Paul VI writes, because each of us has the quality, the ability, the necessary attributes to become a brother or sister to one another. Such confidence he has in human nature, a confidence he does not have to explicitly ask us to share with him.

Paul VI begins to bring his 1971 Message towards a close with a stirring exhortation as valuable in our own time as it was in his: "Whoever works to educate the rising generations in the conviction that every man is our brother, is building from the foundation the edifice of peace. Whoever implants in public opinion the sentiment of human brotherhood without reserve, is preparing better days for the world. Whoever conceives of the protection of political interests without the incitement of hate and of combat amongst men, as a logical and indispensable necessity of social life, is opening to human society the ever-effective advancement of the common good. Whoever helps in discovering in every man, beyond his physical, ethnic, and racial characteristics, the existence of a being equal to his own, is transforming the earth from an epicenter of division, antagonism, treachery and revenge into a field of vital work for civil collaboration."

Paul VI does not make the connection himself, but with his emphasis of "choice of identity" we can find a parallel with the parable of the Good Samaritan, a parable inspired by the question, "Who is my neighbor?" (Luke 10,29-37) It is one of the most familiar of Jesus' parable, telling of a man travelling from Jerusalem to

Jericho. On the way he is attacked by thieves and left for dead. Along come, one at a time, other travelers that might have stopped to help a fellow Jew. They pass by. Then comes a Samaritan, whom the Jews despise, the feelings being generally mutual. He stops to help, tending his wounds and setting him up at an Inn promising to cover all his costs. Though the parable is to be a response to the question "Who is my neighbor," Jesus finishes with a different question: "Who became neighbor?" The parable teaches what Paul VI is calling us to do: choose to become neighbors, to become friends with one another. Paul VI holds we must choose being "a friend" as our personal identity. In doing so, we also become; to borrow the phrase we have seen previously from the Vatican Council II Pastoral Constitution Gaudium et spes, "artisans of peace." (GS no.77)

If Paul VI were, in 1971, to explicitly offer a formula for peace, particularly for peace within a nation, it would no doubt be, "If you want peace, if you want to create peace, choose to be a friend to one another." This 1971 Message, along with the better known 1972 Message, could be my "favorites."

Before moving on, we should take note of two questions he posed earlier in this Message for our prayer and contemplation as he will request in his final 1978 Message. Pessimistically he would have us ponder, "Why, today, does peace recede?" Optimistically we need to reflect, "Why, today, does peace progress?"

1972 – "IF YOU WANT PEACE, WORK FOR JUSTICE"

BACKGROUND 1971

IN VIETNAM, Secretary of Defense Laird announced that *Vietnamization* of the war was ahead of schedule, there being now 334,600 US troops in combat. He also announced an end to *Operation Ranch Hand*, an operation that began in 1962 during the Kennedy administration. Inspired in part by the British use of herbicides in Malaysia in the 1950s, *Operation Ranch Hand* was part of the broader use of herbicides during the war called *Operation Trail Dust*. *Ranch Hand* was the spraying of an estimated 19 million gallons of defoliants and herbicides, at as much as 50 times the concentration of normal agricultural strength, over rural areas of South Vietnam in an attempt to deprive the Viet Cong of both food and ground cover. That these herbicides were dropped in the South, not the North, meant it was not merely the Viet Cong being deprived of food. Some parts of Laos and Cambodia were also sprayed. The most common and recognizable herbicide used was Agent Orange. There were also more toxic agents used: 600,000 gallons of Agent Purple, three times the toxicity of Agent Orange, were sprayed in Laos alone. Nearly 20,000 flights dropping these chemicals were flown by the US between 1962 and 1971, destroying and heavily damaging over 5 million acres of forests and 500,000 acres of crops. The motto of the "Ranch Handers," as the bombing teams were called, was, "Only you can prevent a forest," a rather cynical take on the popular slogan of the US Forest Service's slogan by Smokey the Bear: "Only you can prevent a forest fire."[52] It is to this kind of cynicism, Paul VI's writings suggest, that war brings us as an emotional escape from reality in which we find ourselves.

The South Vietnamese army, with US air support, invaded Laos in February to disrupt the use of the Ho Chi Min Trail as a supply route. The invasion was initially a success but after 45 days of fighting most of the South Vietnamese troops had withdrawn back across the border. Protests in the US and throughout Europe continued to grow. The anti-war organization Weather Underground took credit for a bombing at the US capital on March 1 to protest the Laos invasion. There were no casualties, but the Capital suffered $300,000 in damage. From December 26-28, sixteen members of Vietnam Veterans Against the War occupied the Statue of Liberty.[53] Eighty members of this group were later arrested for staging a protest on the steps of the Lincoln Memorial in Washington, DC. A campaign to obtain amnesty for US deserters and draft evaders continued to grow. On December 30, Daniel Elsberg once again faced indictment on Federal criminal charges related to the release of the Pentagon Papers. By the end of 1971, the number of US military personnel in South Vietnam had been reduced to 156,800.

MESSAGE 1972: - "IF YOU WANT PEACE, WORK FOR JUSTICE!"

An invitation and exhortation:

Men of thought! Men of action!
All mankind living in 1972!
Accept once more
our invitation to celebrate
the Day of Peace!

Paul VI begins his 1972 *Message* noting that, he has "the loftiest conception" of peace," and the idea of peace must be dominant in human affairs. That keeping peace the dominant idea rather than the avoidance of war is as seen a hallmark of his theological approach. He adds that there is an urgency to keeping peace the dominant idea especially "whenever and wherever it is contradicted by opposite ideas or deeds." For this reason, it is "extremely important to have an exact idea of Peace," one that is "free of the false concepts which too often surround and thus deform and distort it."

Not surprisingly, he is speaking "to the young first of all." It is important they they especially keep this "exact idea" dominant in their affairs because, he explains, ideas of peace are too often contradicted by old attitudes and false concepts we carry with us from our past. They young are not yet bothered by the false concepts that distort a genuine idea of peace. They are the best source for the "new attitude" about peace and war for which the Council called in the Pastoral Constitution *Gaudium* et spes. For Paul VI this "new attitude" views peace as "a necessary idea, an imperative idea, an inspiring idea." Peace is an idea that must be defended from such contradictions as "If you want peace, prepare for or make war" that continue to shape government policies. The defense of peace, of an "authentic conception" of peace is "indispensable." He is speaking here of the dangers of settling for the "pretense" of peace to which he has previously referred. The pretense of peace is deceptive, giving the appearance of what does in fact not exist. An example from the pope's perceptive is deterrence, which he insists gives only the pretense of peace. Deterrence might delay a future conflict, creating that "in-between" time, but it cannot establish an authentic peace. Reaching back into the Old Testament he writes "Peace is neither treachery (Cf. Job 15:21), nor a lie made into a system (Cf. Jer 6:14)." Peace is not "a pitiless totalitarian tyranny. Nor is it, in any way, violence." In view of his complete rejection of violence as a means to any legitimate end, it is most interesting that he goes on to pay the compliment that, "at least violence does not dare to appropriate to itself the noble name of Peace."

He again emphasizes that peace cannot be imposed by or in any way coincide with force. These are the opposite and contradiction of an authentic peace. We might think for example of the use of UN "peace keeping forces" to separate belligerents and bring some security to innocent populations. It is not possible to keep peace with force. Such actions in which the UN engages in its role are important but must be seen as a means to an end. These forces should not so much be seen as "keeping peace," but rather as creating the time and space necessary to "establish peace." It happens that people may become too comfortable with or dependent upon this type of peace to move forward, avoiding the necessary reconciliation to which he has previously referred. It happens as well that resentment of or disregard for a peacekeeping presence can result in peacekeepers themselves becoming targets in civil war. In this vein Paul VI speaks directly to those responsible for public order and security, whose "constant temptation" is to impose order by the use of force. To think of peace as the absence of conflict is a powerfully deceptive pretense.

In his UN address, he spoke of an authentic and exact concept of peace somewhat negatively. Here he turns to speak of a positive conception of peace. A "genuine idea" of peace is grounded he writes in a "sincere feeling" people have for one another. And what do we call this sincere feeling, he asks? "We call it Justice." He is confident that a consciousness of justice is increasing throughout the world: "No one, we believe, denies this phenomenon." He credits this to humanity having a new awareness of itself, and the twofold moral movement of rights and duties, his theme in 1969. Just as our understanding of peace must be dynamic, responding to the "signs of the times" as a "work in progress," so too should justice be understood as a "dynamic" taking place "deep in the human heart." An ever-growing awareness of justice "is admissible, is probable and is desirable" he writes. (Note how often the pope speaks in triplets.) This phenomenon of justice as a dynamic of sincere feeling towards others is not that of individuals alone. It is a "collective and universal phenomenon." Recalling his 1967 encyclical *Populorum progressio*, he refers to developing countries that "shout [justice] out with a loud voice. It is the voice of peoples, the voice of mankind." All of humanity demands a new expression of justice as a new foundation for peace. In the face of this "irrepressible cry" he asks the profound question to which all those who love peace must give a ready reply: "Why do we waste time in giving peace any other foundation than Justice?"

Paul VI turns to the Prophet Isaiah, Chapter 32, verse 17 for insight: "It is justice that will bring about peace." He might have cited Psalm 85, 11 to describe the intrinsic, we can even say intimate relationship between justice and peace: "justice and peace shall kiss." Paul VI's 1972 *Message* is an invitation to practice justice as the way to peace. In phrasing found in the French but not the English translation, his *Message* is extended in Latin: *Opus justitiae pax*. "The work of justice is peace." In what he calls a "more incisive and dynamic formula" than offered by Isaiah Paul VI gives us his most well-known expression: "If you want peace, work for justice." Or in deference to his *Message* of the previous year we might rephrase as, "If you want to create peace, create justice." The pope recognizes that his invitation is not without difficulties, "for it always demands some sacrifice of prestige and self-interest." He observes very adroitly that "more greatness of soul" is needed for yielding to the ways of justice and peace than is needed to engage in violence in pursuing one's rights.

As we are accustomed, Paul VI ends on the most positive of notes, writing that he has trust in the power of the ideals of justice and peace to give humanity the moral energy necessary to realize them: "We are confident of their gradual victory." It is by embracing the ideals of justice and peace that we find the motivation to put these ideals into practice. They must first be embraced before they can be realized. He is more confident still that "modern man has an understanding of the ways of peace, sufficient to enable him to become a promoter of that Justice." Holding to a pretense of peace will not bring about justice. Just as deterrence cannot bring about authentic peace, neither can it contribute to bringing about justice. Quite the opposite. The sums of economic resources needed to build a military deterrent will always deprive those in need of those resources justice demands for them. It is only with an authentic understanding of peace that we can become promoters of justice with a "courageous and prophetic hope. That is why We dare once again to extend an invitation to celebrate the Day of Peace," with the added reminder that "if we want peace, we must work for justice." January 1 can also be referred to as a celebration of the Day of Justice.

4
1973 - 1978

"You must serve the cause of peace, and not make use of it for aims other than the true aims of peace."
PAUL VI

1973 – "PEACE IS POSSIBLE"

BACKGROUND 1972

IN VIETNAM, PRESIDENT NIXON COMMITTED THE US TO LEAVING A RESIDUAL FORCE of 25,000 to 35,000 in South Vietnam after the completion of the *Vietnamization* of the war. New Zealand, Australia, and Thailand withdrew their forces. In March the North, which had walked out of the Paris talks, launched a massive invasion of the South with the Easter Offensive. As with the previous Tet Offenses, this incursion failed to bring them a final victory, but it did inflict upon the US and South Vietnamese staggering casualties undermining US resolve. Ultimately though, it was not so much military engagement that moved to North to negotiate as concern that Nixon's policy of détente towards the Soviet Union and China might undermine their crucial support in the war. After the "failure" of the Easter Offensive the North entered secret negotiations outside the prevue of the Paris Talks with the US. After the Easter Offensive, the US was determined to leave Vietnam sooner rather than later. To that end, these negotiations excluded the South who would in turn become an obstacle to a "separate peace."

Secretary of State Henry Kissinger led the negotiations. Among the terms negotiated were the North's commitment after the end of hostilities to not invade the South, allowing that government to remain in place while negotiations for a political solution to the conflict took place. There were to be free and democratic elections to determine the South's future. The North also gained such favorable terms as retaining all territory it had captured as well as, over the objections of the South, the withdrawal of all US troops. No residual force would be left behind, as had been previously promised, to assist the South in enforcing these terms. The US would however continue to provide air support and the provision of armaments.

When South Vietnamese President Nguyen Van Thieu learned of these terms, he was understandably angry at being left out of the negotiations and demanded changes more favorable to the South's security and territorial integrity. To pressure Thieu to accept the terms, the North again stepped back from talks and made public some of the details. Feeling that the North was trying to embarrass him by exposing the growing rift between the US and the South over details to end if not the war than US involvement in it, and wanting the war resolved whatever it took, Nixon ordered a resumption of US bombing with Operation Linebacker II. Over the course of 12 days, beginning on 18 December, the last major military operation by the US in Vietnam unfolded. Known as the Christmas Bombings and reminiscent of the December bombings of 1967 that so angered the pope, the largest bombing campaign since World War II dropped more than 20,000 tons of ordnance on military and industrial targets in Hanoi and Haiphong, killing at least 1,624 civilians.[54] Paul VI publicly deplored the bombing in his weekly general audience on 20 December, expressing his "painful emotion over the sudden renewal of harsh and heavy military operations in blessed Vietnam, which has become a cause of daily grief."[55]

MESSAGE 1973: – "PEACE IS POSSIBLE!"

At the time he composed his 1973 *Message* he would not have known of the bombing campaign to take place on the very eve of its publication. Given the scope and breadth of the Vatican's diplomatic connections it is possible he was aware of the possibility of an end to hostilities, which may explain why his 1973 Message may be the most optimistic of the collection. He begins with what many might say is a somewhat whimsical picture of a future world at peace. Allow me to provide several quotes: "Wisdom has finally triumphed; weapons are still and are rusting in the armories, useless instruments of a madness...Worldwide and serious institutions guarantee safety and independence to all. International life is organized by now undisputed documents and instruments which immediately work to solve, through a listing of rights and justice, every possible controversy. Dialogue between peoples is continuous and sincere and, in addition, an immense intertwining of common interests brings about solidarity among peoples."

He boldly concludes, "Peace has now come to civilization!" This is a peace that should be neither doubted nor called into question "by those with a more cynical perspective." It should be "embraced unconditionally."

The year 1973 provides the opportunity to take the concerns and interests of peace in new direction, with new questions to be asked and answered. Empathically he asserts, "Peace is a fact, peace is secure; it is no longer a matter for discussion!" Then it's back to reality with what feels like whiplash.

"Really?" he ponders? "Would that it were so!" Using the biblical clothing metaphor, he laments that "violence becomes fashionable again, and even clothes itself in the breastplate of justice." Paul VI is troubled by attempts to justify violence as a remedy for injustice. This openness to violence as a justifiable means to establish justice will be of particular concern to him within the Liberation Theology movement in Central and South America in his 1975 Apostolic Exhortation, *Evangelii Nuntiandi*, as previously noted. People seem no longer horrified by crime and cruelty, which he describes as "the surgery of hate," seemingly becoming if not legal and acceptable, at least tolerable. Genocide is again viewed as the "possible monster of a radical solution." He has in mind here no doubt the Holocaust of the past, and somewhat prophetically those genocides to come: the Cambodian genocide that would begin in just 2 years' time; the Rwandan genocide of 1994; the Srebrenica genocide in Bosnia & Herzegovina in 1995 during which more than 8,000 Bosniak Muslim men and boys were killed.[56] Demonstrating his awareness of the breadth of the challenges the world faces in achieving peace, he notes that behind these events lies, with "thorough, cold-blooded and unerring calculations, the huge economy of arms, with its hunger-producing markets." In such an environment we might join him as he asks, "can peace survive?" "Yes Peace!" he insists. "Peace can survive!" Not only can peace survive but "in and to some extent [peace can] exist side by side with the most unfavorable conditions of the world." Whether in the fighting or the pauses of war, even "amid the ruins of all normal order," there are quiet corners and quiet moments to be found. "Peace," he writes, "immediately adapts itself to them and, in its own way, flourishes." Do we seek them out?

Still, he wonders returning to a previous theme, "Shall we give the name of peace to its counterfeits?" He quotes the Roman military historian Tacitus as offering just such a counterfeit: *Ubi solitudinem faciunt pacem appellant*: Where they make solitude, they call it peace."[57] Can the name peace be assigned to a truce, to "a mere laying down of arms?" Was the armistice of November 11, 1918, worthy of the name peace, he might have asked. Does the name peace properly belong "to a temporary balance of opposed forces," to a balance that consists of nothing more than the "immobile tension of rival powers?" Can nuclear, or any kind of military-based deterrence, be "worthy of the title peace?" He has spoken of the "pretense" of peace. He now refers to "impostures" of peace. There is a prevailing hypocrisy, that of wanting peace through force, which he laments has been seen throughout history. It is such hypocrisies that lead to the notion that "If you want peace," you must prepare for, make or threaten war. There are those who believe that a kind of peace can be achieved even in precarious and unjust situations. This notion sees peace as entailing the necessary compromises to attain "a fragile and partial settlement, a diplomatic balance and regulation or rival interest." Nothing more is possible they say: "man is made to fight against man: *homo homini lupus*. War is inevitable."

Paul VI acknowledges that in Scripture it is the sword that comes first, and only after the ploughshare (Isaiah 2,4), and he observes that too often a perceived need for the sword overwhelms the true need for the ploughshares. This is true "even for some developing peoples, which are struggling to enter into modern civilization." Nations that can least afford to "needlessly take on enormous sacrifices in the resources that are essential for life's basic needs, of food, medicine, education, the building of housing and roads" for the sake of armaments. There is even the sacrificing of "true economic and political independence" for the sake of possessing arms. So much sacrifice "so that they can be armed and can inflict fear and slavery on their own neighbors. There is little thought of offering friendship, cooperation, a common well-being." The pope warns that these counterfeit attitudes and sacrificing what is of true value for human betterment in favor of armaments give rise to doubt about the possibility of peace, "a doubt that could be fatal." In the face of these challenges, we must cling to the conviction that genuine peace is possible, and not disturb that conviction by calling it into question. Paul VI challenges us to not question the possibility of peace, but to instead affirm its possibility, setting aside any doubts we may be tempted to harbor so we can begin to address the new and original questions for the betterment of humanity to which he alluded earlier.

His closing thoughts, his plea deserves to be quoted at some length: "Let us not allow the idea of peace to perish, nor the hope of peace, nor the aspiration towards it, nor the experience of it, but let us renew the desire for peace in men's hearts, at all levels: in the inmost sanctuary of consciences, in family life, in the dialectic of social conflicts, in relations between classes and nations, in the support of initiatives and international institutions that have peace as their banner. Let us make peace possible by preaching friendship and practicing love of neighbor, justice and Christian forgiveness."

If we want peace, we must not doubt peace. Instead, we need to hold fast to our conviction in the possibility of peace, a possibility the foundation of which is "not that of brute force, but that of love." As with each year previous we can discern a new formula to capture his insights and challenges: "If you want peace, want to create peace, believe peace is possible!"

1974 – "PEACE DEPENDS ON YOU TOO!"

BACKGROUND 1973

IN VIETNAM, Nixon informed Thieu that the US would sign the treaty Kissinger had negotiated with North Vietnam with or without his agreement. He wanted the war over and saw this as an opportunity to leave quickly and, or so he thought, "with honor." To help encourage Thieu to accept the treaty Nixon sent South Vietnam $1 billion in military equipment. With this aid, the South Vietnamese air force became the fourth largest in the world. He promised continued military and economic aid and made a commitment to reintroduce US forces in South Vietnam should North Vietnam violate the agreement to not invade. Reluctantly, Thieu dropped his objections. On January 15 Nixon announced the end of all offensive operations against the North. Former President Johnson passed away at his Texas ranch just a week later, January 22. Five days after the former president's death, January 27, the *Paris Accords* were signed. The last of the US troops departed on March 29, 1973.[58]

MESSAGE 1974: – "PEACE DEPENDS ON YOU TOO!"

Seeing at last the ending of US military involvement in Vietnam must have been for Paul VI a moment of some satisfaction. As described in Volume 1, the unique relationship between himself and President Johnson was key to the unprecedented role in modern times of a pope playing a pivotal role in bringing belligerents together. John XXIII played an unprecedented though indirect role in helping to resolve the Cuban Missile Crisis by way of a public appeal to everyone's "better angels." Paul VI played a direct role in bringing the US and North Vietnam to the negotiating table, but doing so by his owns choice behind the scenes. It might be suggested that although officially ignored at the time, his personal letters to all the leaders of belligerent nations in the early years of his papacy may have planted a seed of credibility in North Vietnam that made the behind the scenes possible. This seed was watered and tended by both his public criticisms of the war, especially of the bombings, his two Marian encyclicals in which he addressed aspects of the war, and his sending Vatican sponsored humanitarian aid to the

North as well as the South while calling on international Catholic aid organizations to do likewise.

Paul VI begins his Message in an almost apologetic manner. This is the seventh time he has gone to his global audience. Twice he asks, "Listen to me again," before confessing, "Naturally, as you will have guessed, I wish to speak to you once more about Peace." He wonders aloud, "Perhaps you think you know all there is to be known about Peace; so much has already been said about it by everybody. Perhaps this obtrusive term provokes a feeling of satiety, of boredom." "Perhaps also," he goes on, "of fear that it conceals behind the charm of its name an illusory magic, an abstruse and over-indulged rhetoric, even a dangerous spell." His readers might wonder if his optimism has diminished since his first Message in 1968. The world has continued to see, he once again observes, international conflict, class warfare, coups and military juntas, civil wars and revolutions, the abuse and denial of basic human rights and worldwide economic instability. History seems intent on presenting the idea of peace "as if it were the statue of an idol." The prospects for peace seemed grim as humanity appeared to be "a permanently insoluble problem of living self-conflict, a being who bears in his heart the destiny of fraternal strife."

In the face of these realities Paul VI nevertheless writes that he continues to possess "an indomitable idealism." In his self-reflecting wonderment whether he were a Hamlet or a Don Quixote, in matters of peace he is the Quixote: Peace is "destined for progressive affirmation...We are so convinced that Peace is the goal of mankind in the process of its growing self-awareness and of the development of society on the face of the earth, that today, for the new year and for future years, we dare to proclaim, as we did last year: Peace is possible!"

In his 1973 Message he mentioned that doubts about achieving peace pose a significant danger to peace. Such doubts, he writes, give rise to counterfeit ideas of peace that are a kind of hypocrisy. In 1974 he speaks of a different danger: "the unspoken and skeptical conviction that, in practice, Peace is impossible." A "wonderful idea" and an "excellent synthesis of human aspirations" perhaps, but in the end an authentic and genuine peace is nothing more than "a poetic dream and a utopian fallacy." However beautiful a concept, the idea of peace has for some, especially for some world leaders, become akin to "an intoxicating drug." The inevitable logic of such thinking is "the thought that what matters is force." The best that can be hoped is that humanity will reduce the combination of forces to a balance of opposition: arms reduction. Many will come to the conclusion that "organized society cannot do without force," and will settle for somehow managing that force in such a way as to miss the peace of *Shalom, Eiréné* and *Pax*, settling instead for *pas*, the peace of which there is nothing more than the absence of violence.

Paul VI emphasizes that peace must not be confused with weakness, neither a physical nor and more importantly a moral weakness. Nor can peace be equated "with the renunciation of genuine rights and equitable justice." Peace does not allow anyone who claims to be committed to peace to as it were "sit this one out." Similarly, the "If you want peace, appease" to avoid conflict is contrary to achieving an authentic peace. Peace must not be confused with "avoiding risk and sacrifice...This is not real Peace." Cowardice in the face of injustice is not any more peace than is appeasement or a settlement imposed by fear. "True peace," as he reminded his readers by noting the Twenty-fifth Anniversary of the *Declaration of Human Rights* in his 1973 *Message*, must be grounded in the "untouchable dignity of the human person from which arise inviolable rights and corresponding duties." Paul VI is recalling to mind the theme of his 1969 *Message*, "If you want peace, promote and defend human rights." The pursuit of peace "will never be without a hunger and thirst for justice." "Blessed are those who hunger and thirst for righteousness," the pope might have reminded us from the Sermon on the Mount, "for they shall be satisfied:" they shall have peace. (Matthew 5,6). Similarly, those pursuing peace will do so, "never losing sight of the efforts that must be made to defend the weak and the poor, and "to promote the cause of the lowly." In some his strongest language that peace does not allow passivity but demands nonviolence, he insists, "Peace will never betray the higher values of life in order to survive (cf. Jn 12: 25)." Genuine peace will never yield to a static keeping of an established order with an attitude of "don't rock the boat." On the contrary, peace will always hold to a dynamic search for the equilibrium of which he has spoken, whatever the discomfort or the cost of personal sacrifice.

In emphasizing the dynamic nature of peace, he cautions against thinking that peace is some reality to which we can point and say, "here it is, we have it now." He may be borrowing the concept of the presence of the *Kingdom of God*, as described in the Gospels. To neither peace nor the Kingdom of the Prince of Peace can we say, "'Here it is' or 'there it is.'" (Luke 17,21) Like the Kingdom of God, Peace is not a matter of a static "being" to which one can point, but of a dynamic "becoming." As seen earlier, it is not so much that we "enjoy" peace he taught us, but that we "create" and "invent" peace. It is not enough to have a conviction of the necessity of peace. Humanity must see the pursuit of peace as a duty, a duty that "takes hold of conscience as a supreme ethical objective, as a moral necessity," even in the face of opposition. There can be no "sitting this one out" in the pursuit of justice and peace: If we want peace, it is our duty to work for justice.

Paul VI knows well the cynicism he faces: "Can you not see - any observer could object - that the world is moving towards conflicts even more terrible and horrible than those of yesterday? Can you not see the lack of effectiveness of propaganda for peace and the insufficient influence of the international institutions that were set up while the bloodied and weakened world was recovering from the World Wars? Where is the world going? Are not ever more catastrophic and abhorrent conflicts being prepared?"

He ponders whether he ought to remain silent in the face of such "pressing and implacable reasoning." His emphatic response is not unexpected: "No, we are certain that our cause, the cause of Peace, must prevail." He goes on to explain why.

Firstly, Paul VI maintains that "the idea of Peace is already victorious in the thought of all men in posts of responsibility. We have confidence in their up-to-date wisdom, their energy and ability...No head of a nation can wish for war." Motivated by such confidence, "We dare to exhort leaders never again to deny their program, indeed the common program of Peace."

A second reason he offers is the power of the idea of peace itself. If the idea of peace truly wins humanity's hearts, "Peace will be safe." If peace is safe, he maintains, "it will save mankind." He speaks of the power of ideas in shaping public opinion and its influence on the actions of world leaders, suggesting that the thought of Peace is "the queen" that rules over peoples' thoughts and actions, the "imponderable influence" shaping public opinion which in turn, he suggests, shapes and rules over the thinking and actions of world leaders.

Finally, Paul VI posits that, "If public opinion is the element that determines the fate of the Peoples, the fate of Peace also depends on each person." Here he comes to his central message: "This is what we wished to say: Peace is possible, if *each one of us* wants it; if *each one of us* loves it." [emphasis added] In a way reminiscent of his homily at Yankee Stadium in 1965, Paul VI is directing his words personally to the "individual." Not noticeable in the English, but in the French translation we can see that he does not here use the second person plural (*vous*) but the singular "you" (*tu*). Peace is possible if "each one of us educates and forms our own outlook to Peace, defends peace, works for peace." Perhaps he is recalling the commemorative medal commissioned to mark his visit to UN in 1965 with the inscription *Amoris alumna Pax*: "Student of love and peace." The medal cast for this historical event does not use the plural *alumni*, but instead the singular *alumna*. To obtain and embrace this medal was not to join a band of "students" of peace, but to identify oneself as a "student" of peace. The Council referred to "artisans" of peace. Paul VI here is calling for the "artist." The medal, as this year's *Message*, captures Paul VI's "impelling call" to "each one of us" who wants and loves peace to never lose sight of the fact that, "Peace depends on you (each individual) too." Peace depends on me too. Paul VI maintains that while the influence of any one person on public opinion may seem "infinitesimal," it is never in vain. Instead, "Peace lives by the support, though individual and anonymous, that people give it." His principal message may be that of the duty of "each of us," but the duty does not stop there. The support each of us gives to the commitment "must progress from being individual to being collective and communal," an affirmation of each one of us and of all of us. The student moves towards students, the artist towards arcticians.

He brings his Message to its conclusion writing: "This is what we venture to say to you...You must give to your action a strong and wise orientation towards Peace. Peace has need of you... Peace depends also and especially on you." Going back to the Introduction of this present work, we might here recall the formula, "If you want peace, it is your duty to work for peace." To paraphrase what he himself asserts, "Peace has need of you, of us, *of each one* of us."

1975 – "RECONCILIATION, THE WAY TO PEACE"

BACKGROUND – 1974

IN VIETNAM, fighting continued across the South. The terms of the Paris Peace Accords signed the previous year were of no effect. Nixon's promise of continued support for the South was as shallow as the commitment of the North to the Accords. No aid was forthcoming. The oil embargo initiated by the Organization of Arab Petroleum Exporting Countries (OAPEC) against countries that had supported Israel during the Yom Kippur War in October 1973 had put the US in a position of needing to conserve its own oil reserves at home leading to a curtailing of supplies of fuel to South Vietnam. Military support to the South was also curtailed. With limited resources, the South was forced to adopt an increasingly untenable defensive position with continued loss of morale amongst its armed forces. It was not long before the geographical perimeter of South Vietnam was being reduced to the capital Saigon and the Mekong Delta.

In June, US Defense Attaché to South Vietnam, General John E Murray, informed the Pentagon that South Vietnam required a minimum of $1.26 billion to replenish its military supplies to defend itself. He went on to indicate that $900 million in aid would merely slow the South's military decline after mid-1975. $750 million in aid would be insufficient for the South to stop a major attack, such as was seen with the Tet and Easter Offenses. He concluded that with$600 million the US should "write off South Vietnam as a bad investment and broken promise."[59]

MESSAGE 1975: – "RECONCILIATION AS THE WAY TO PEACE"

Paul VI continues to speak in the new year of peace as a "created tranquility" of the equilibrium found in a balancing various parties' interests, doing so with dynamic new language: "Peace must become *operative* and *wise*. Peace must be *produced*; Peace must be *invented*." [emphasis added] Institutions and organizations dedicated to the cause of peace can succeed only "if they are continually active, if they know how to *generate* Peace, *make* Peace at every moment." [emphasis added] Peace becomes *operative*, is *made, produced* and *invented* he stresses through reconciliation.

As noted in his 1970 *Message* on the similar theme, reconciliation comes to us from the Latin *reconciliare*, meaning to bring together or to become friendly again. In acknowledging the difficulties in achieving peace he repeats his observation from his 1970 *Message* that reconciliation is perhaps the most difficult of all the pathways to peace he has until now described. But just as he never sees a link between peace and war, so too he has never seen a link between the difficult and the impossible. Peace is not some "fantasy" meant to distract us from the troubles of the world. He is not "playing at utopias." As always, he is determined to "remain in the realms of reality," realities in which there tragically remains the possibility of "more terrible fatal clashes" than have been experienced in the past. Of still greater concern to him is the reality that conflict and war is thought by some, including theologians in South and Central America, to be "in certain circumstances, inevitable and necessary, and called for, as it were, by justice."

Paul VI rejects any notion that violence can be a path to justice. Imagine if you will Martin Luther King, Jr. or Ceasar Chavez, both of whose commitment to nonviolence Paul VI lent is public support, embarked on campaigns of violence in the pursuit of civil and labor rights. Having written in 1972, "If you want peace, work for justice," he now poses a most frightening question he credits to St Augustine: "Will justice be one day the sister no longer of peace but of wars?" Could it be that justice and peace will no longer kiss (Psalm 85,11), but instead make fists?

A singular event leading up to 1975 can be identified as informing Paul VI's decision to return to the theme of reconciliation as well as to speak again to the issue of nonviolence. Both issues were very much on his mind going into the new year. His concern to emphasize nonviolence in the pursuit of justice be said to stem from his work on his 1975 Apostolic Exhortation *Evangelii Nuntiandi*, "Proclaiming the Gospel," following from the 1974 Synod of Bishops. Paul VI had convened this, his third of four Synods after instituting the synodal process at the suggestion of the bishops at the Vatican Council in September 1965 prior to the Council's close in December of that year. Paul VI wanted the bishops to explore in 1974 the topic of evangelization in this new age on the occasion of the tenth anniversary of the Vatican II "Pastoral Constitution on the Church in the Modern World," *Gaudium et spes*. It was the original expectation that the Synod of bishops would prepare a document the pope would then use in writing an Apostolic Exhortation. At this Synod however, the bishops were not able to agree on a final text due to the "maneuvering" of the Cardinal Archbishop of Krakow, Poland and future Pope John Paul II. As a result, "everything was simply dumped in the papal lap, and Paul was invited to sort it all out."[60] The result was Paul VI's "last and finest Apostolic Exhortation," *Evangelii Nuntiandi*, described as "a work of discernment and synthesis."[61]

Discussed in some detail in Volume 1, Paul VI began his exhortation by emphasizing the importance and necessity of nonviolence. He did so in the context of Liberation Theology, especially in South and Central America, which he felt lent itself to the idea that violence could be justified in some circumstances, such as liberation from oppression. In response he insists, "The Church cannot accept violence, especially the force of arms...and indiscriminate death as the path to liberation, because she knows that violence always provokes violence and irresistibly engenders new forms of oppression and enslavement which are often harder to bear than those from which they claimed to bring freedom." (*EN, 37*) He then quotes himself from two addresses he gave while in Columbia in 1968: "We exhort you not to place your trust in violence and revolution: that is contrary to the Christian spirit, and it can also delay instead of advancing that social uplifting to which you lawfully aspire...We must say and reaffirm that violence is not in accord with the Gospel, that it is not Christian; and that sudden or violent changes of structures would be deceitful, ineffective of themselves, and certainly not in conformity with the dignity of the people."[62] Clearly, the rejection of any idea that violence can ever be embraced in any circumstance and his embrace and affirmation of nonviolence was on Paul VI's mind when putting pen to paper for his 1975 Peace *Message*.

That he would return to the theme of reconciliation in 1975 reflects also the vision he had for that year, announced three years prior on January 27, 1972, that 1975 would celebrate an Extraordinary Holy Year.[63] Paul VI declared 1974 to be a "Holy Year of Preparation" in his Apostolic Exhortation *Pater cum benevolentia*, "Father of Benevolence." 1975 would be a Holy Year of "Reconciliation Within the Church," a year for the Church to celebrate "the happiness that we enjoy in reconciliation with Christ, who is our peace." His *Peace Message* of reconciliation was "a complement" to the Apostolic Exhortation emphasizing the need within the Church for her members to be reconciled with God and especially one another. These personal reconciliations within the Church, so necessary after the upheaval from the reforms of the Council, were to be a witness to the need for reconciliation among nations. Here is found the distinction between his 1970 and 1975 *Messages*: 1970 was a universal call for reconciliation among nations whereas 1975 had an emphasis on the reconciliation needed amongst Catholics rooted in the chaos and confusion that followed the implementation of the reforms of the Second Vatican Council. It was only after much soul searching that he ultimately decided to take the risk that a Holy Year could be a time of healing and not further antagonize the wounds the Church suffered during his papacy.

Although the documents of the Council were adopted by the bishops by overwhelming majorities, conservative quarters in the Church who voted against them, particularly the Declaration on Religious Liberty, *Dignitatis Humanae*, continued their opposition during the time of implementation of the Council's reforms. Chief among them was the French Archbishop Marcel Lefebvre who rejected, among other reforms, the liturgical reforms grounded in the "Constitution on the Sacred Liturgy," *Sacrosantum Concilium*. In 1970 Lefebvre founded the Society of Pius X to train seminarians to celebrate the Tridentine Mass, The Mass "of the Council of Trent," codified by Pius V in 1570.[64] Paul VI suppressed this liturgy with the introduction of the "Mass of Paul VI," also known as the novus ordo, the "ordinary form" of the Mass in 1969.[65] The Mass with the new Roman Missal and the Divine Office for priests and religious were introduced to the faithful in 1970.[66]

Discontent had also expressed itself after the closing of the Council from progressives in the Church. In 1967 he disappointed many with his encyclical *Sacerdotalis Caelibatus*, "On Priestly Celibacy," in which he upheld the Church's traditional teaching on mandatory celibacy within the ordained priesthood.[67] He further disappointed progressives in 1968 with his encyclical *Humanae Vitae*, "On Human Life," in which he upheld the Church's traditional ban on the use of artificial means of birth regulation. This was the pope's last encyclical of the remaining ten years of his papacy and perhaps is the best example of the tension that persisted throughout those remaining ten years. He wanted, then, the Holy Year of 1975 to be a time to "perfect the sense of our unity – unity *in* the Church – unity *of* the Church." It was also to be, citing the Council's "Decree on Ecumenism," *Unitatis redintegracio*, a time to pray for Christian unity as well as to engage in dialogue with other religions so that "we may collaborate for world Peace." His 1975 *Peace Message*, with its singular theme of reconciliation *in* and *of* particular communities and nonviolence, was given in service to the success of the Holy Year.

Paul VI begins his *Message* with the challenge of his theme: "Reconciliation! Young men and women, strong men and women, responsible men and women, free men and women, good men and women - will you think of it? Could not this magic word find a place in the dictionary of your hopes and of your success?" Referencing *Gaudium et spes* at paragraph 82, he states his *Message's* "characteristic and inspiring point." He insists humanity needs to embrace a spirituality of peace saying, "Peace only has value to the extent that it seeks first to be interior before becoming exterior." Before humanity can move away from arms that inflict physical harm, the human spirit itself must be disarmed. He continues, "It is not enough to contain wars, to suspend conflicts, to impose truces and armistices, to define boundaries and relationships, to create sources of common interest; it is not enough to paralyze the possibility of radical strife through the terror of unheard-of destruction and suffering." He calls these a type of utilitarian and provisional approach, insufficient to achieve genuine peace. Progress must be made "towards a Peace which is love, free and brotherly, founded, that is, on a reconciliation of hearts." Without this reconciliation of hearts, "man will prefer," he writes quoting from St Augustine, "to be with his dog rather than with a man who is a stranger. (cf. De Civitate Dei, XIX, VII; PL 41, 634)." Even if reconciliation is the most difficult of any path to peace, "it is not impossible; it is not a fantasy."

It is interesting that Paul VI takes the opportunity in a *Message* whose theme is reconciliation he acknowledges the UN declaration of 1975 as the *International Year of the Woman*. As noted in his inaugural *Message* in 1968, the pope tends to avoid mixing celebrations and anniversaries. Nevertheless, in 1975 he "rejoices" at the increased participation in and the important and expanding role woman play in society.[68] Paul VI himself greatly expanded the role of women in the Church, such as his inclusion of women on the *Pontifical Birth Control Commission*. He makes a point to acknowledge, and I do hope no one sees this as patronizing or sexist but only as sincere, the qualities of intuition, creativity, sensibility, compassion, and a capacity for understanding and love that woman possess that enables them to be "in a very particular way creators of reconciliation in families and in society." In a similar way he acknowledges what he calls the "new universal mentality of human oneness" possessed by the youth of the world. The world's youth have "a mentality which is not skeptical, not vile, not inept, not oblivious of justice, but generous, and loving." They possess "unforeseeable resources for reconciliation." The combined capacity for reconciliation possessed by both women and the youth can be signposts "on the road of Peace we travel in truth, in honour, in justice, in love," giving hope of a "new history of mankind."

"This then," Paul VI concludes, "is our message of good wishes for you: reconciliation is the way to Peace." With the previous years we can attribute to him the formula, "If you want peace, pursue the path of reconciliation." With this 1975 *Message*, as in several years, there is a prophetic element to this formula.

Ten years after Paul VI's 1975 *Message* some nations began formal investigations of civil rights abuses and war crimes at home to hold accountable those responsible and to facilitate and make possible a people's reconciliation with one another and their past. There is the beginning of an international movement of nations seeking to make, produce and invent peace with themselves. There have been fifty such commissions between 1983 and 2021, the most up to date information I was able to track. The most well know perhaps is the Truth and Reconciliation Commission established after the end of apartheid in South Africa in 1995. The Commission was led by Archbishop Desmond Tutu who was awarded the Nobel Peace Prize for his role in the opposition to apartheid in 1984.

The best-known examples in South America would be those commissions that followed the military dictatorship, the "Dirty War," in Argentina from 1974 to 1983,[69] and the government sanctioned "death-squads" in El Salvador from the early 1960's until the end of the civil war in 1992.[70] Examples in the US include the 2004-2006 investigation of the Greensboro Massacre, Greensboro, North Carolina, of November 3, 1979,[71] and the 2012-2015 "Maine Wabanaki-State Child Welfare Truth and Reconciliation Commission" which investigated events related to the removal of Wabanaki children from their homes and culture, and led to passage of the Indian Child Welfare Act in 1978.[72]

The track record of these commissions is mixed. The most successful and recognized is the "Truth and Reconciliation Commission" in South Africa. Some of the testimony of victims of apartheid was given in public hearings. On the other end of the spectrum is the 1982 "National Commission of Inquiry into Disappearances" in Boliva, the first of a series of Latin American commissions. The Commission never completed its report. On September 6, 2023, the British parliament gave final approval to a bill that both ended all ongoing investigations of human rights abuses during *The Troubles* in Northern Ireland (late 1960's-1998) and prohibited any further public inquiries into those abuses. The legislation goes further in prohibiting any compensation to victims of government military action, and grants amnesty to perpetrators of violence against Catholics by Protestant militias and government troops.[73] The law does not conform to the norms established by the European Commission on Human Rights which, for example, holds that granting amnesties is incompatible with the state's obligation to provide effective investigations of killings and possible torture.

1976 – "THE REAL WEAPONS OF PEACE"

BACKGROUND 1975
IN VIETNAM, Hanoi declared the 1973 Paris Peace Accords to be "null and void" and began a massive invasion of the South in March. The US promise of military support by Nixon was not kept by the new President, Gerald Ford, who succeeded Nixon upon his

resignation August 8, 1974, in the wake of Watergate. The South Vietnamese army quickly fell apart. A final attack on Saigon began April 29, and the city was taken by the afternoon of the 30th, and the Socialist Republic of Vietnam was born. In the days and hours before the fall of Saigon nearly all American civilian and military personnel were evacuated in Operation Frequent Wind, the largest helicopter evacuation in US history. There were no US ground troops in the South under the terms of the Paris Accords to assist in the evacuation. Some few Americans chose not to be evacuated. It was 30 April 1975 that the two decades of US involvement in Southeast Asia centered around Vietnam, fiercely opposed by Paul VI, came to an end. There was now a united Vietnamese peninsula,. The names of the 58,267 US casualties are forever remembered from that war on the National Mall in Washington, DC on the Vietnam Memorial Wall.[74]

We might note here, considering the US support of the Cambodian Kingdom and involvement in Cambodia as part of its war efforts in South Vietnam, that 1975 also saw the end of the 5-year Cambodian civil war. The victorious Communist Khmer Rouge now governed the new Democratic Kampuchea. So began a campaign of state-sponsored genocide. It is estimated that more than one million Cambodians were murdered in what came to be known as the "Killing Fields." Estimates of the total deaths resulting from Khmer Rouge policies, including death from disease and starvation, range from 1.7 to 2.5 million out of the 1975 population of roughly 8 million. The genocide continued until 1979 when the Socialist Republic of Vietnam invaded, bringing an end to the Khmer Rouge government and the genocide.

MESSAGE – 1976: "THE REAL WEAPONS OF PEACE"

In his 1976 Message, Paul VI seeks to flip war on its head, making the absence of war a byproduct or side-effect of creating peace rather than the definition of it. We can say that his insight here is that if we promote human rights, seek reconciliation, and work for justice, we will achieve peace and war will disappear. We do not eliminate war to have peace. War will disappear on its own if we create, invent, produce, and make genuine peace. Hence, he will shift our linguistic use of the term "weapons," adopting the term for the achievement of peace as the term's military significance will in time become obsolete. He is anticipating the day when the term no longer has meaning unless redefined. With appeal once again to the metaphor of Isaiah 2,4, Paul VI believes that swords, weapons of war, can be repurposed into ploughshares, becoming now weapons of peace. Using these "weapons" he urges, "Let us not refuse any sacrifice which...will make peace quicker, more heartfelt and more lasting." In marking the 10th anniversary of John XXIII's encyclical *Pacem in terris*, he goes on to expresses trust that with our "weapons of peace," "the memory of that great flame which he [John XXIII] kindled in the world will strengthen hearts to new and firmer resolutions for peace." His *Message* he says is simple: "Peace is possible!" Peace is possible he writes if it is truly willed. Further, it must be willed because willing peace is a duty. It is our duty to will peace in our time: if we want peace, we must recognize our duty to will it.

In this *Message* he warns of "a disproportionate growth...of the possession of arms of every kind, in every individual Nation" driven by the arms race that has resulted from a reliance on deterrence as a pathway to peace. He shares his "justified suspicion" that because of the reliance on deterrence, the arms trade "often reaches the highest levels in international markets." He describes as "fallacious and deceptive" any notion that defense, "even if it is planned as something purely hypothetical and potential," will result in anything more than the stand-off of opposing military balances. "Is this Peace? Is it civilization?" In rather stunning language he asks, "Can we give the name People to a mass of citizens who are opposed one to another to the bitter end?" There must be a different kind of defense other than that achieved by building a stockpile of armaments."

A peace which is merely a truce or armistice is "a precarious peace indeed." He goes on to site as another hypocrisy "a tranquility which is called peaceful only with cold words of simulated reciprocal respect." "Poor Peace!" he laments. "What then are your weapons?" Such a peace has only the "Fear of unheard-of and fatal conflagrations, which could decimate, indeed almost annihilate humanity?" Returning to language used in his UN Address in 1965, he warns against a "Resignation to a certain state of endured oppression, such as colonialism, imperialism or revolution." Each begins as violence "and inexorably becomes static and terribly self-perpetuating?" He makes a most interesting reference to nations possessing a "self-absorbed bewitchment," or as in the French translation a certain "narcissism" (*narcissisme*) that breeds a culture that is "presumptuous and convinced of its own perennial triumphant destinies?" This exaggerated sense of self-importance and destiny can, and has, led to an extreme and dangerous nationalism such as seen in Nazi Germany of the past and today with the rise of the Alternative for Germany party (AfD), as well as with Marie Le Pen's National Rally party in France. The White Supremacist Movement in the US similarly fits Paul VI's description of the dangers to peace. "Poor peace" indeed if its only weapons are those "destined to kill and exterminate mankind."

What are needed both then and today are "moral weapons, those which give strength and prestige to international law." By speaking of strength from "moral weapons" Paul VI distinguishes himself from Pius XII who trusted that it was necessary that international law be enforced by an international authority. The first of these moral weapons of peace is fidelity: faithful observance to international treaties. He insists that the fundament principle of "agreements must be kept" remains a valid international norm. This principle is of such importance he refers to it as "peace's shield." As he did at the UN, he praises both international organizations and international treaties that seek to prevent war through negotiation and mediation.[75] These are the moral weapons needed for peace. This man of dialogue sees dialogue as a powerful tool to prevent war, more powerful than a defense based on deterrence.

Whereas governments speak of "unilateral disarmament," one side disarming as a sign of good faith to entice the other side to follow suit, and more often of "bilateral disarmament" with each party only acting in concert with another, Paul VI speaks of "judicious disarming" as another moral weapon of peace. He quotes again the prophet Isaiah's call to turn spears into plowshares. He adds another Scripture, this one offering not a metaphor like Isaiah but a practical command first given to the Apostle Peter in the Garden of Gethsemane when Jesus is arrested, a command Paul VI sees as binding on all of humanity: "Put your sword back, for all who draw the sword will die by the sword' (Mt 26:52)." As with Paul VI's pathways to peace offered in the annual Messages, Jesus' words can likewise be said to survive and go past their own particular moment in time.

Paul VI does admit, in referencing St Paul's letter to the Romans 13,4, that traditional weapons of war such as the sword have had a place in the pursuit of justice and peace. Still, he dares to ask, "has there not come into the world a transforming dynamism, a hope which is no longer unlikely," that humanity will go beyond agreements to limit the ability to destroy life? His hope, "no longer unlikely hope," is that humanity will move beyond simply living by the old Law, "'You have learnt how it was said to our ancestors: 'You must not kill,'" towards a new and radical embrace of the common good of refusing to harbor anger (Mt 5:17, 21-22)."[76] This is a new law," which arms peace with the formidable principle, 'You are all brothers.' (Mat 28:8)" From here he easily segways to the idea that nonviolence is an important "moral weapon" of peace. He offers the Indian pacifist and patriot Mahatma Ghandi as an example of what can be done, armed as he was with only the principle of non-violence to bring about "the freedom and dignity of New People." He will again hold-up Ghandi as an example to be followed of non-violence in an address on All India Radio to mark the thirtieth anniversary of his assassination on January 30, 1978.

There is but one more weapon to offer: the olive branch, "which civilization carries in a procession of a justice completely intent on defending the weak, punishing the violent and ensuring an order" that can rightly be called "peace." "Let us rejoice this procession," a procession of justice, even if it is "interrupted by hostile attacks (what today we refer to as acts of terrorism) and by unexpected accidents." (Can we be forgiving?) This procession must continue "along its way before our eyes in this tragic time of ours!" Continuing the poetic metaphor he writes, "Its step is perhaps a little slow, but it is nonetheless sure and beneficial for the whole world." Truly, "It is a procession intent on using the real weapons of peace."

Were Paul VI to explicitly give us a new formula for peace in 1976 it might be, "If you want peace, take up the moral weapons of peace:'" fidelity to agreements, judicious disarmament, nonviolence, and a readiness to offer to one's enemy the olive branch.

1977 – "DEFEND LIFE"

1976 BACKGROUND SOUTHEAST ASIA:

The new Socialist Republic of Vietnam began a "re-education" of citizens of the former South Vietnam, which included mostly former government officials and military officers. Also caught up in these programs were many doctors, lawyers, and other intellectuals. In neighboring China a bloodless coup overthrew the short-lived rule of the Gang of Four in China led by Chairman Mao Zedong's widow, Jiang Qing, after the Chairman's death on September 6, 1976. A military coup and subsequent massacre in Thailand on the evening of the October 6 installed an ultra-right government.

MESSAGE – 1977: "IF YOU WANT PEACE, DEFEND LIFE!"

Paul VI begins his 1977 *Message* with an acknowledgement: "Here we are again, for the tenth time, speaking with you! At the dawn of the new year 1977, we stand at your door and knock (Rev.3,20) Please open to us." He describes himself humbly as the "usual Pilgrim travelling the roads of the world without growing weary or losing the way." He is speaking from literal experience, having made nine pilgrimages to six continents, twenty nations from Jordan in 1964

68

to Ceylon in 1970, experiencing one assassination attempt along the way.[77] In this role, he sees himself as a "prophet of peace," come to announces a new reality. Still with that same humility with which he spoke at the UN 12 years previous, he hopes that his audience will "not think our annual message on behalf of peace superfluous and therefore boring." Is he losing confidence that anyone is still listening? No, not from a lack of confidence. He speaks on behalf of peace from a genuine spirit of humility.

He notes as he has in the past the spirit of peace that followed World War II, the spirit that peace at long last seemed victorious. He describes the works and institutions dedicated to peace that emerged after the war as, in his own poetic way, "fresh spring leaves." There can be no civilization without peace he writes, observing as well that peace "is never complete, never truly secure." This incompleteness and insecurity are the result of peace suffering from the re-emergence of conflicts only "provisionally settled," what he has previously described as giving the "pretense" of peace, as well as the appearance of new conflicts. He sees a progression in the sufferings of peace, emerging "first in people's feelings, then in partial and localized disputes, and then in frightening programmes of armament." It is true that "here and there" can be found "praiseworthy attempts" to avert war, but these are insufficient. He reminds insightfuly that "Peace does not generate itself," but depends on us to create and invent it. Again, using poetic metaphors, he describes peace as like a flexible body "that needs a stout skeleton to give it strength," and again, "that the pyramid of Peace should have a solid base and a lofty summit."

As he has written in previous years, peace cannot be seen as a dream, neither as a utopia nor illusion. Most importantly perhaps, peace must not be thought of as an exercise in futility; it is not "a labour of Sisyphus."[78] He repeats his refrain that peace is possible, quickly qualifying, "let us be sincere:" peace is possible "only with the concourse of many and not easy conditions." The examination of these conditions he will, for the most part, leave "to the experts." Still, "We shall not be silent on one aspect, one which is clearly of basic importance:" that of having a deep appreciation for the relationship between peace and life. Peace and life "are supreme values in the civil order." In a way similar to the relationship used to describe the relationship of peace and human rights in his 1969 *Message*, he speaks of peace and life as "interdependent." "Do we want peace?" he asks. "Then let us defend life!"

He acknowledges that throughout history the relationship between peace and life has often reflected more a "fierce struggle" than a "fraternal embrace," such as he described between peace and justice in 1972. He assures his readers he will offer no empty "rhetorical slogan." When peace is sought and thought to be won through conflict, life is put at risk and sacrificed. Even in the necessity of self-defense, he points out, "life is sacrificed for the sake of peace." However contrary to logic it may seem, "Peace and Life can in practice be dissociated." He will go on to label this idea a "reprehensible hypothesis."

Interestingly I think, in light of my commentary on Paul VI's motivations related to bombing in Vietnam presented in Volume 1, he makes appeal to the atomic bombing of Hiroshima to illustrate his assertion that life and peace can be and has been "disassociated" from life. The loss of hundreds of thousands of Japanese lives by the Allied bombing, more than 100,000 in the incendiary bombing of Tokyo alone,[79] in service to ending the war is juxtapositioned with that bombing, especially that of Hiroshima and Nagasaki, being in service to the saving of Allied lives by eliminating the need for a ground invasion. In some of his strongest language found in his *Messages*, he refers to this dissociation as a "reprehensible hypothesis." For Paul VI, it is "reprehensible" to hold any notion that peace and life should be so disassociated from each other as to suggest that peace is possible only through "a sad triumph of death."[80] He repeats the quote, differently translated, of the Roman historian Tacitus: "'They make a desert and call it Peace.'"

In what might be characterized as a nod to the reality of what Parchami called a "loose" interpretation of peace discussed above, and reflective of his 1967 encyclical *Populorum Progressio*, Paul VI includes in his harsh assessment of this hypothesis the notion that "the privileged Life of some can be exalted, can be selfishly and almost idolatrously preferred, at the expense of the oppression or suppression of others." The way forward requires us to recognize "the primacy of Life as a value and as a condition for Peace." As he did in 1972, he again explicitly offers his "formula" for peace: "'If you want Peace, defend Life!'" Going beyond John XXIII's judgement that it is no longer "reasonable" to think of war as a pathway to peace, this pope asserts that, if we hold that life is sacred, "*war is virtually disqualified* as a normal and habitual means of asserting rights and so of ensuring Peace." [emphasis added] Who but a pope, who but Paul VI can with moral authority pronounce war as "virtually disqualified as a normal and habitual means of asserting rights...of ensuring peace." In what he calls "the final analysis, Peace is...the joyful celebration of Life."

Before concluding, he expands his "if you want peace, defend life" formula to express three imperatives. To have an "authentic and happy peace" it is not only necessary to defend life, but also to "heal" and "promote life." With that thinking as a foundation for peace, "The policy of massive armaments is immediately called into question." The ancient and contemporary maxim seen in Chapter 1, *si vis pacem, parabellum* - "if you want peace prepare for war," "is not acceptable without radical reservation." Such a "radical reservation" he suggests can be found in Jesus' reference to the king who stops to re-think a decision to go to war. (Luke 14:31).[81] Continuing his use of strong language he continues, "With the forthright boldness of our principles, we thus denounce the false and dangerous programmme of the 'arms race,' of the secret rivalry between peoples for military superiority." Not surprisingly he follows this denunciation of the arms race with a word to "praise the effort already begun to reduce and finally to eliminate" what he terms a "senseless cold war."

Paul VI then broadens his theme to make the point that "it is not only war that kills Peace. Every crime against life is a blow to

71

Peace." He again laments that offences against life seem to have come to be accepted, tolerated as "normal behavior."[82] The crimes of individuals are now "organized to become collective." This is turn ensures the silence and complicity of whole groups of citizens, allowing private vendettas to become "a vile collective duty." Speaking as if prophetically, he speaks of terrorism emerging as a legitimate political strategy. Police torture, and here we might think of the so-called "enhanced interrogation" techniques such as the use of waterboarding after 9/11, are viewed as effective means of "imposing ignoble repression," that is to say, reducing a person to such a state helplessness, rather than establishing and maintain right order.[83]

We can certainly add here the seeming ease in the US with which gun violence is tolerated, even when the victims are children and their teachers in their school classrooms. To quote the Director of the US Centers for Disease Control and Prevention, Dr Rochelle Walensky, gun violence in the US has become "a serious public health threat."[84] Hate speech, bullying, and the dissemination of disinformation and conspiracy theories over social media are said to be protected by the First Amendment right to free speech.[85] Peace cannot flourish "where the safety of life is compromised in this way." Where violence begins, true peace ends. In contrast, "where human rights are truly professed and publicly recognized and defended, Peace becomes the joyful and operative atmosphere of life in society." In his own words is the challenge: "Do we want Peace? Then let us defend Life!"

1978 – "NO TO VIOLENCE, YES TO PEACE"

BACKGROUND 1977:
The Socialist Republic of Vietnam continued to consolidate its power in the south, bringing with it the socialist reforms that had governed the north. It would be the following year, 1978, that the government would begin to nationalize industry and commerce and set prices for commodities. These policies led to a decline in industrial output

and commerce, and to widespread poverty. Collective farming was also introduced, leading to widespread food shortages. The government set prices for fertilizer, seed and farming equipment that were out of reach for most of the agricultural community leading a further decline in agricultural production, widespread hunger and rationing. Although many Vietnamese from the South began to flee the country soon after the fall of Saigon in 1975, thousands more began to flee beginning in 1978, coming to be known throughout the world as the "boat people."[86]

MESSAGE 1978: "NO TO VIOLENCE, YES TO PEACE!"

In what would be his final *Peace Message*, Paul VI declares that peace to consists of "an intelligent and living courage." This expression is packed with insight and challenge. The notion of "intelligent courage" is by itself worthy of the contemplation to which we are called in this *Message*. He wants in this *Message* to "beseech...all men and women of good will:" Then he drills down: "the leaders of the collective conduct of the life of society, politicians, thinkers, publishers, artists, those who mould public opinion, the teachers in the schools, the teachers of art, of prayer, the great planners and..." not to leave anyone out: "operators of the world arms market - we beseech all of them to begin once more to reflect with generous honesty on Peace in the world, today!" One might first think that by "today," he means New Year's Day, January 1, 1978. In the context of these *Messages* as a whole, as well as by this time being very familiar with his train of thought, it is perhaps best to think of his use of "today" as implying a sense of urgency. The time embrace an "intelligent and living courage," "to reflect with generous honesty on peace" must be "today!" There is no time to lose in the pursuit of peace. A fitting *Message* for Paul VI to bring his yearly insights full circle.

He begins by commenting on two phenomena he sees emerging in the world. The first is the progress peace is making in the hearts and minds and lives of humanity, a phenomenon he describes as "magnificently positive." As he has in previous *Messages*, we find him using both liturgical and poetic language: "The history of our time - let it be said for its glory - is studded with the flowers of a splendid documentation in favor of Peace." He refers to the upcoming *First Special Session of the United Nations General Assembly Dedicated to Disarmament* but does not mention his invitation to speak on this occasion, an invitation to return thirteen years after his first Address. If it is true as has been suggested he "wrangled" his invitation in 1965, this second invitation from Secretary-General Kurt Waldheim is a clear demonstration of the respect Paul VI earned amongst the world community in his peace efforts in the years following his call for "War never again!" Not only the first pope to address the UN, but to do so twice, a second visit about whom few seem to be aware. Not even biographer Hebblethwaite mentions it. It speaks more directly to the importance his insights and exhortations on disarmament had taken on, an issue as seen in Volume 1 on which he broke new ground in the Catholic Social Justice tradition. He accepted the invitation to once again address the UN although he did not address the General Assembly in person. He was represented on June 6 by Agostino Casaroli, Secretary of the Council for the Public Affairs of the Church.[87]

Within the context of this "magnificently positive" phenomenon, he posits that "No one today dares to defend as principles of wellbeing and of glory deliberate programs of murderous strife between men, that is, programs of war." He expresses confidence, again using strong language that goes beyond John XXIII's expression that war is no longer a "reasonable" option, that the choice of armed conflict, "which today as never before is *insanely murderous and destructive*," [emphasis added] can be avoided. He maintains that "the conscience of the world is horrified by the hypothesis that our Peace is nothing but a truce," such that an "uncontrollable conflagration" could break out at any moment. He goes on that he "would like to be able to dispel this *threatening and terrible nightmare*," an expression he has used in other texts to express the psychological impact of the appeal to nuclear deterrence, "by proclaiming at the top of Our voice the absurdity of modern war, and the absolute necessity of Peace." [emphasis added] In the instance of emphasis we need note he is not metaphorical with the term "nightmare." This pope on several occasions pushed the tradition forward on the evaluation of nuclear weapons. Whereas noted in Volume 1 his predecessor Pius XII made a quantitative evaluation of the destructive power of such weapons, which made their use for him suspect, it is Paul VI who moves the tradition solidly to a qualitative evaluation of their possession. He took seriously and integrated into Catholic thought the psychological impact of nuclear weapons which grounded his unprecedented and even in some Catholic theological circles lonely position that the mere possession of these weapons could not be morally justified. He confirms his literal sense of "nightmare" as he continues to emphasize that a genuine and authentic peace cannot be founded on the power of weapons and their "infernal destructive capacity." In speaking of this "infernal destructive capacity," he has in mind the first uses of the atomic bomb in Japan. His reference to the events of 1945 of three decades previous, and especially by reminding readers that Hiroshima was bombed on date of August 6, for him spiritually important date the Catholic Church celebrates the *Solemnity of the Transfiguration*, lends credibility I hope to my explorations of his motivations for his particular attention to the strategy of bombing in Vietnam, discussed in Chapter 6 in Volume 1.

Paul VI returns as if to summarize in 1978 to familiar themes. Peace cannot be founded on nor enforced by political tyranny, but must instead be founded "on the patient, rational and loyal method of justice and freedom." This is, he says in yet another nod to the importance of the UN, the approach promoted and defended by "the great international institutions of today." Paul VI seems to never miss an opportunity to reinforce the confidence he has in international organizations to achieve peace, a confidence first expressed in his UN thirteen years prior, and which will be repeat for the last time in his address of June 6 to the Special Session on Disarmament. No pope before him, not even John XXIII, held and spoke of such organizations as the UN in such esteem. This is perhaps because he is very much a man and pope of dialogue, and places like the UN are those in which dialogue, conversation; not bombastic and accusatory, self-righteous rhetoric; can and should take place. Referring to his predecessors Pius XII, who supported the UN but saw no role for the Church in it, and John XXIII who before his election as pope encouraged such engagement, Paul VI, who in 1964, the first full year of his papacy, had appointed a permanent observer from the Vatican to the UN, expresses the hope that the "combined teachings" of the popes "will continue to inspire...the wisdom of modern teachers and contemporary politicians." As seen previously in this present work, John XXIII with his encyclical *Pacem in terris* was the strongest inspiration for him. In view of the advances he brought over the teachings of Pius XII, such as conscientious objection discussed in detail in Chapter 3 of Volume 1, I can only wonder if he refers to Pius XII here more out of a sense of the loyalty he always gave to this pope than any of his teachings on peace.

The second phenomenon is the negative: "passionate and premeditated violence." He is speaking here not of international conflicts but of those between individuals and groups in society, and his language is direct and forceful, and we can even say graphic. There is a prophetic sense in his final *Message*: "This phenomenon is spreading in modern civilized life; is taking on alarming proportions, to the extent that it is becoming habitual." There are individuals and groups who, due to prejudice, bigotry, extreme nationalist beliefs, ignorance, and tribal differences, engage in "passionate and premeditated violence" against others in their own country. In an almost prophetic way he anticipates the hate, racist, homophobic, anti-Sematic, anti-Muslim and anti-immigrant attitude and crimes -the list goes on - that plague our own nation today.[88] He seemingly anticipates the violence against, for example, Asians because of COVID.[89] He offers that "Often the psychology of violence takes its origin from the depraved root of deliberate revenge." We might speak today of such a "psychology of violence" in the context of the "radicalization" of individuals who come to embrace a violent politics or ideology. As this violence spreads and, as he notes, becomes habitual society becomes numb and unresponsive, a topic addressed in the previous year. We have moments of "silence" when Paul VI would call for non-violent resistance and progress.

The pope describes this violence as an "explosion of a blind energy" that not only injures its victims, but also degrades those who perpetrate it. He sees an aspect of violence "that has been made into a system 'for settling accounts.'" Does not this violence, he asks, "have recourse to contemptible forms of hatred which imperil society and shame the community" Again, there is a somewhat prophetic aspect to this notion of settling accounts in the US with the rise in the US of "revenge porn," also known as image-based sexual abuse and nonconsensual pornography, as revenge for a breakup in a relationship as well as in cases of attempted blackmail.[90]

The pope makes the interesting observation that these and similar types of violence are antisocial "by reason of the very methods that allow it to be organized into group complicity." He sees "a conspiracy of silence" that forms "the binding cement and the protective shield" for the crime. The result is what he insightfully and somewhat creatively calls a "palliative of conscience," a conscience that is, literally, "covered over," recognizing no sense of responsibility to give a voice, to speak out and to advocate for the victims. His Message here is reminiscent of the words of Proverbs 31,8, "Open your mouth for the mute, for the rights of all who are destitute." He speaks of distortions "of the true social sense, a distortion which clothes with secrecy and with the threat of pitiless revenge certain associated forms of collective selfishness." This type of violence "is always clever" at evading normal legal processes, much like the serpent in Genesis 3,1. Such criminal undertakings are he suggests, "the final result of a wrong choice of road and the cause of deplorable forms of repression."

He ends this discussion of individual and social violence with the admonition that it is well for us to recall Christ's admonition that, "'all who take the sword will perish by the sword (Mt 26: 52). We must remember that violence does not ennoble those who have recourse to it."

Up to now, "In this Message of Peace we are speaking about violence as the antagonistic term of Peace, and we have not spoken about war." He returns to that theme now as war "still deserves our condemnation." As with his immediate predecessor John XXIII, Paul VI uses the term "condemnation" sparingly and with deliberation. He allows that the idea of war is more widely rejected than in the past, writing that "against it a praiseworthy and ever more authoritative effort is being made, both socially and politically." Still, and here he returns to the notion of deterrence, war "is being kept in check by the terrible nature of its own arms." This is not peace, but rather simply the fear of war, an observation seen often in his writings. With deterrence, it is fear that "holds in check the eventuality that war might turn into a cosmic conflagration." This fear is more "an imagined restraint than a real one." He is nevertheless able to put a somewhat positive spin on the arms race by suggesting it may not be as much a balancing the forces as an acknowledgement of "the *supreme irrationality* of war." [emphasis added] The nations of this world, all of humanity must move beyond this irrationality "towards establishing relationships between Peoples, which are ever more interdependent...ever more friendly and human." His prayer: "God grant that it be so!"

I have suggested that it might be wondered if Paul VI intuited that this would be his final *Message*. Part of that wonderment is that it is at this time that he turns his attention not just to youth of this world, but specifically to children: "We must add a word for all the children. About violence, they are the most vulnerable sector of society, but they are likewise the hope of a better tomorrow." It is his hope that through a thoughtful intermediary his Message might "reach them to."[91] He offers three reasons to explain why he has such a hope for an intermediary to speak to children, reasons that show, for all his lack of pastoral experience aside from his years as archbishop of Milan (1954-1963), he possesses keen pastoral instincts.

Firstly, as he has pointed out in previous *Messages*, he does not speak in his own name, "but only but in the name of Christ, the 'Prince of Peace' in the world (Isaiah 9: 6)." He then refers to the Sermon on the Mount which proclaims, "Blessed are the peacemakers, for they shall be called children of God' (Mt 5: 9)." This might be coupled with the Scripture in which Jeus says that it is to those who receive the kingdom "like children" that this kingdom of God belongs." (Mark 10,14-15) The message of peace must be passed on to children who will then witness to what we as adults hope to establish: "stable and universal peace." It is only true peace that makes us "capable of struggling for justice and of settling very many questions with the generosity, indeed the genius, of love."

The second reason is that, although children and youth often quarrel, it is important for them to be taught "it is a harmful vanity to want to appear stronger than your brothers and sisters and friends by quarrelling, fighting, and giving way to anger and revenge." If they want to be strong, they need to be so "in spirit and in behavior." It is necessary that the young learn to control themselves, learning how to forgive and quickly make friends again with those who have offended them." Here he is asking adults to pass on to children the lessons of his 1970 and 1975 *Messages* of reconciliation. In a call for respect for the diversity of humanity Paul VI calls on children, calls on us, to not hate anyone. Everyday should be a day like that described by a policeman on the day the pope visited New York in 1965: a day when "nobody hated nobody." Children need to be taught to not be proud, "not comparing yourself with others of your own age, with people from different social backgrounds or with people of different nations." Comparing only leads to them, to us, acting "out of selfish motives, out of contempt or - we repeat, of revenge."

In his third reason, he places his hopes for a better more peaceful future in their care. He places his trust in the young to live the "new attitude" of which the Council spoke in *Gaudium et spes* about peace and war. His words are spoken directly to them: "We think that when you grow up you must make a change in the way today's world thinks and acts, a world in which everyone is always ready to be different, to be separate from others and to fight. Are we not all brothers and sisters? Are we not all members of the same human family? And are not all the nations obliged to get on well together and to create Peace?"

For there to be peace "children of the new age" must get used to loving everyone and to giving society an ideal of community which is "more noble, more honest, and more unified" than the one they have inherited. If children and the young, indeed all of us, truly want to be human rather than "wolves:" "If we really want to experience the joy of doing what is right, helping those in need, and of being able to do good works with the sole reward of a good conscience, we must remember the words which Jesus spoke at the Last Supper: 'A new commandment I give to you, that you love one another... By this all men will know that you are my disciples, if you have love for one another (Jn 13: 34-35).' This is the mark of our authenticity, our humanity, our Christianity: that we love one another."

As I have said, I find it difficult to read his 1978 *Message* without thinking he knew it would be his last. His last words in a *New Year's Message* carry for us then a degree of profound importance: "Dear children, we greet you and we bless you. The password [to the future] is: No to violence, Yes to Peace." Were we to dare offer a tagline from this, his final and perhaps most personal of all his speeches and writings, it might be with the Evangelist, "If you want peace, love one another with actions an in truth." (1 John 3,18)

FINAL REFLECTION

Over the course of the two volumes of *Pope Paul VI and His Quest for Peace 1963-1978* I have researched, explored and written a great deal about, in Volume 1, and commented upon, in Volume 2, the person, papacy, deeds, speeches and writings of Paul VI. He is often referred to as the "Pilgrim Pope" for his travels, and the "First Modern Pope" for his bringing to completion and implementing Vatican Council II. Having gone into such depth about this one central dimension of his papacy and legacy it may be difficult to appreciate how it is he is also known as the "forgotten pope." Yet so he is.

That he was the first pope to leave Italy in 1964 since 1809, the first to do so in more than a century and a half, is nevertheless "forgotten" by some who refer to his successor John Paul II as having claim to this honor.[92] In a recent interview I had for my first book, *Striving to be Perfect as the Heavenly Father is Perfect*, I made reference to the fact that I had taken a break from writing this work about Paul VI to write something more personal. In the TV presentation of the interview, it was noted I had taken a break from a book about "Pope John Paul VI!"[93] I am not sure what happened to the III – V! In many ways the individuals and papacies of "Pope John" and "Pope Paul" have become lost in the outsized papacy of "Pope John Paul II." Paul VI can be said to be the more forgotten of the two. He is in good company though: another pope who sought world peace, Benedict XV of World War I, has also been designated by some Church historians as a "forgotten" pope.[94] I believe the 60th anniversary of Paul VI's historic pilgrimage to New York to address the UN, a pilgrimage during which he called for "no more one against the other" and "Never again war," a day which a member of New York's finest described as one on which "nobody hated nobody" is the most appropriate time to bring him, his efforts and his message of peace back from the abyss of the forgotten to the focal point of remembrance. Neither for his sake nor the sake of his legacy do we do this, certainly, but for our sake, for the sake of our future.

If we want peace...what? How do we think? How do we act? How do we respond to international threats, bullying, terrorism, sexual assault, the denial of civil rights and so much more? What is the pathway to peace? The obvious and indisputable answer to peace is beautifully, profoundly and often prophetically articulated in life, speeches and writings of Paul VI. There are many issues over which Paul VI agonized during his papacy, but the subject of peace was not one of them. He may have wondered to himself if he were a Hamlet or Don Quixote, but when it came to peace Paul VI approached the subject without any "Hamletesque" hesitation. He did so from day-one with the optimism and idealism of a Don Quixote; with the spirit and commitment, the confidence and faith of a Saint.[95]

In marking the 60th anniversary of his address to the United Nations by recalling the place of peace in his papacy and heart, we recognize that his messages of peace survive and go past their own particular moment in time: peace is not an absence of conflict, but a presence of fruitfulness, justice, respect for life and human rights, of reconciliation and nonviolence. Peace is a reality that is imaginable, definable, tangible, accessible, attainable. In short, peace is possible; difficult he often reminds us, but possible. Of all that Paul VI demonstrated about peace in his papacy, I would close by suggesting it is his central message that peace is not some far off concept "blowing in the wind." Paraphrasing the Book of Deuteronomy 30, 11-14, Paul VI's enduring message: is that peace is [Peace is] *"not too difficult for us or beyond our reach. It is not up in heaven, so that we must ask, 'Who will ascend into heaven to get it and proclaim it?' Nor is it beyond the sea, so that we must ask, 'Who will cross the sea to get it and proclaim it?' No, peace is very near to us, it is in our mouths and in our hearts."* "May peace among men triumph!" PAUL VI, VATICAN COUNCIL II , SEPTEMBER 14, 1965

Select Bibliography for Volumes 1 and 2 of Pope Paul VI and His Quest for World Peace 1963-1978

Abbot, Walter, The Documents of Vatican II, Guild Press, NY 1966.

Adamo, Salvatore J., "The Anguish of the Pope," in Paul VI: *Critical Appraisals*, James F. Andrews, Edito, Bruce Publishing, New York 1970, pp. 29-40.

Adler, Bill; Ross, Sayre, *Pope Paul in the United States*, Hawthorn Books, New York, NY 1965.

Allen, John L. Jr., "Remembering Paul VI, the Superhuman." National Catholic Reporter, online at ncr.org, August 8, 2008

Andrews, James F., "The Pope in an Age of Insecurity." In *Paul VI: Critical Appraisals*, James F Andrews, Editor, Bruce Publishing, New York, NY 1970, pp.7-28.

An Instrument of Your Peace: Official Documentary of the Visit of His Holiness, Pope Paul VI, to the United Nations and New York, Edward T. Fleming, Editor, Curtis Publishing, Philadelphia, PA 1965.

Anon., "Paul VI Planned US-Backed Peace Mission for Vietnam." *National Catholic Register*, April 29, 2001, vol.77, no.17, p.5.

Archdiocese of Baltimore, President, *Lady Bird Johnson had long association with Catholics*, online at archbalt.org, January 19, 2012.

Aubert, Roger, *Catholic Social Teaching: An Historical Perspective*, David A. Bolieu, Editor, Marquette University Press, Milwaukee, WI 2003.

Andrew, James F., General Editor, Paul VI: Critical Appraisals, Bruce Publishing, New York 1970.

Barrett, William E., *Sheperd of Mankind: A Biography of Pope Paul VI*, Double Day & Company, Garden City, NJ 1964.

Benedict XVI, "Paul VI's contribution to the Church becoming increasingly evident." *Catholic News Agency*, online at *catholicnewsagency.com*, April 21, 2022.

Berg, A. Scott, Wilson, G.P. Putnam's Sons, New York, NY 2013.

Bergman, Roger, "Conscientious Objection to Unjust War." *Journal of Religion & Society: Supplemental Series*, number 14, The Kripke Center, Creighton University, Omaha, NB 2017.

Billington, Monroe, "Lyndon B. Johnson: The Religion of a Politician." JSTOR, vol.17, no.3, pp.519-530.

Brivio, Ernesto, *The Life and Miracles of St Carlo Borromeo*, Veneranda Fabbrica del Duomo di Milano, Italy 2006.

Borromeo, Charles, "'Will you risk your life for your flock?' Homily to Superiors of Monasteries and Other Religious Priests at the Time of the Plague, 1576," in *Sermons in Times of Crisis*, with introduction and commentary by Rev. Paul D. Scalia, TAN Books, Charlotte, North Carolina 1964, pp. 61-67. (This homily was among those sent by Paul VI to the bishops of the Vatican Council II before the Second Session in 1964.)

Charles Borromeo: Selected Orations, Homilies and Writings, John R. Cihak, Editor, Translated by Ansgar Santogrossi, Bloomsbury Publishing, London, UK 2017.

Clancy, John G., *Apostle for Our Time: Pope Paul VI*, P.J. Kennedy & Sons, New York, NY 1963.

Collins, Michael, *Paul VI: Pilgrim Pope*, Liturgical Press, Collegeville, MN 2018.

Cooney, John, *The American Pope: The Life and Times of Francis Cardinal Spellman*, Dell Publishing Co., New York, NY 1968.

De Cesare, Raffaele, Trevelyan, George Macaulay, The Last Days of Papal Rome: 1850-1870, Kessinger Publishing, Whitefish, MT 2010

Dewart, Leslie "Peace and the Papal Witness." Chronical (no publication information given), pp. 126-129.

Dick, John Alonzo, Jean Jadot: Paul's Man in Washington, AnotherVoice Publications (no location given) 2021.

Ditewig, William T., "The Pope at the UN: This Month and 50 Years Ago." The Priest, October 2015, vol.71, no.10, p. 31.

Duffy, Eamon, *Saints & Sinners: A History of the Popes*, Yale University Press, New Haven, CT 2015.

Ebrel, Jason T.; Ostertag, Chrsitopher, "Conscientious Refusals in Health Care." online at *chausa.org/publications*, Winter-Spring 2020.

Editorial, "The Pope and Peace." *The Christian Century*, 1968, vol.85,no.1, p. 3.

Fabert, Andre, *Pope Paul VI*, Monarch Books, Derby, CT 1963.

Fiske, Edward B., "The Reign of Pope Paul: A Brief History." *The New York Times*, August 7, 1978, Section A, pages 12ff.

J.L. Gonzalez, J.L.; Perez, T, *Paul VI*, English Translation by Edward L. Heston, C.S.R., St Paul Press, Boston, MA 1964.

Goodwin, Doris Kearns, *Leadership in Turbulent Times*, Simon & Schuster, New York, NY 20018. See: Chapter 12, "Visionary Leadership: Lyndon Johnson and Civil Rights," pp.306-343

Goodwin, Doris Kearns, *Lyndon Johnson and the American Dream*, Thomas Dune Books, New York, NY 2019.

Gregg, Chrissy, "The Destruction of Monte Cassino." online at *Nationalww2museum.org/war/articles*, January 15, 2021

Gremillion, Joseph, The Gospel of Peace and Justice: Catholic Social Teaching Since Pope John, Orbis Books, Maryknoll, NY 1976.

Guitton, Jean, The Pope Speaks: Dialogues of Paul VI with Jean Guitton, English Translation by Anne and Christopher Fremantle, Meredith Press, NY 1968.

Hapgood, David; Richardson, David, *Monte Cassino: The Story of the Most Controversial Battle of World War II,* Da Capo Press (no location given) 2002.

Harris, Ruth-Ann Mellish, *The Great Famine and the Irish Diaspora in America*, University of Massachusetts Press, Amherst, MA. 1999;

Hastings, Max, Catastrophe 1914: Europe Goes to War, Alfred A. Knopf, New York, NY 2013.

Hebblethwaite, *Peter, Pope John XXIII: Shepherd of the Modern World*, Doubleday & Company, Garden City, NY 1985

Hebblethwaite, Peter, Paul VI: The First Modern Pope, Paulist Press, NY 1993.

Hrynkow, Christopher, "'If You Want Peace, Work for Justice:' Pope Paul VI A Peacebuilder on the Levels of Insight and Action." *Peace and Conflict Studies*, 2017, vol.24: no.2, Article 2.

Imbelli, Robert P., "The Transfiguration of Humanity (Homage to Paul VI)," online at *Thecatholicthing.org*, April 21, 2022.

Johnson, Lyndon B., February 1967. "The President's Reply to a Message from Pope Paul VI on Vietnam." online at *The American Presidency Project, presidency.usb.edu*, February 8, 1967.

Jones-Nosacek, Cynthia, "Conscientious Objection, Not Refusal: The Power of a Word." *The Linacre Quarterly*, 2021, vol.88, no.3, pp. 242-46.

Loftus, Eleanor P., Pope Paul VI (1963-1978): Reconciliation, the Way to Peace, PhD Dissertation, Duquesne University 1998.

Magliano, Tony, "Pope Paul's encyclical: Kings speech more relevant than ever." online at *National Catholic Reporter – BLOG*, "Making a difference," May 2, 2017.

Mayor, Stephen, "Development Is the New Name for Peace." *Reformed and Presbyterian World*, September 1968, vol.30, no.3, pp.114-119.

McAndrews, Lawrence, "Agents of Change: Lyndon Johnson, Catholics and civil rights." In, Andrews, Lawrence, *Politics and the Religious Imagination*, Taylor & Francis, Oxfordshire, UK 2010, available at eBooK ISBN *9780203849224*.

McAuley, Joseph, "The Transfiguration of Paul VI." online at americamagazine.org, August 6, 2015.

McNamara, Robert S., "Preface," In Retrospect: The Tragedy and Lessons of Vietnam, Vintage Press Publishers, New York 1996.

Miller, Donald L., Masters of the Air: America's Bombers Who Fought the Air War Against Nazi Germany, Simon and Schuster, New York, NY 2006.

Mishra, Amaresh, *War of Civilizations: India 1857 AD* (vol 1): The Long Road Revolution, India 1857; *War of Civilizations: India 1857 AD (vol 2): The Road to Delhi*, Rupa & Co., India 2007.

Montini, Giovanni Battista, *Man's Religious Sense: A Pastoral Letter to the Ambrosian Diocese*, The Newman Press, Westminster, MD 1961.

Montini, Giovanni Battista, The Christian in the Material World, Helicon Press, Baltimore, MD 1963.

Montini, Giovanni Battista, The Church, Helicon, Baltimore, MD. 1964

Nixon, J. Peter, "Why Paul VI is the saint we need right now." online at *uscatholic.org*, October 4, 2018.

Nuclear Disarmament: Key Statements of Popes, Bishops, Councils and Churches, Robert Heyer, Editor, Paulist Press, Ramsey, NJ 1982.

O'Malley, John W., *A History of the Popes: From Peter to the Present*, Sheed & Ward, New York, NY 2011.

O'Malley, John W., "Papal Upgrades: How did the popes become so powerful?" *America Magazine*, July-August 2011, pp. 38-41.

Passelecq, Georges; Suchecky, Bernaes, *The Hidden Encyclical of Pius XI*, Translated from the French by Steven Rendall, Harcourt Brace, New York, NY 1997.

"Pope Paul VI: Former Supreme Pontiff of the Roman Catholic Church." online at *archives.org/details/humanrightsinnovators*.

Parchami, Ari, *Hegemonic Peace and Empire: The Pax Romana, Britannica and Americana*, Routledge Publishers, London, UK 2009.

Paul VI: Fourteen Hours: A Picture Story of the Pope's Historic First Visit to America, Introduction by Francis Cardinal Spellman, Dell Publishing Company, New York, NY 1965.

Philpot, Terry, "World War I's Pope Benedict and the pursuit of peace." online at *nationalcatholicreporter.org*, July 19, 2014

Edward H. Pitts, "Peace, Paul and Mary." *Christianity Today*, October 14, 1966, vol.11, no.1, pp.49-51.

Pope Paul VI: Christian Values and Virtues, Introduction by Karl A. Schultz, Editor, Crossroad Publishing, New York, NY 2007.

Rose, Gideon, *How Wars End: Why We Always Fight the Last Battle*, Simon & Schuster, New York, NY 2011.

Rothman, Lily, "The First Time a Pope Visited the U.S. Was Much More Complicated." *Time*, September 21, 2015, online at *Time.com*.

Russell, John Quinn-Isodore, "Abandoning the Crown: U.S.-Vatican Relations During the Vietnam War, 1963-1968." *Senior Thesis Seminar*, Department of History, Columbia University, New York (no date).

Serafian, Michael, *The Pilgrim*, Farrar, Straus and Company, New York, NY 1964.

Spellman, Francis J., *No Greater Love: The Story of Our Soldiers*, Charles Scribner's Sons, New York 1945.

Staff Members of *The New York Times, The Pope's Journey to the United States*, A.M. Rosenthal and Arthur Gelb, Editors, Herder and Hebridean, New York, NY 1965.

Thomas, Cooper, *Bombing missions of the Vietnam War: "A visual record of the largest aerial bombardment in history: 1965-1975, online at storymaps.acrgos.com/stories.*

Trentmann, Frank, *The Germans: 1942-2022*, Knopf Publishing, New York, NY 2004.

United States Catholic Conference, Statement on the Catholic Conscientious Objector, online at usccb.org, October 15, 1969

Watkins, Kevin, "Cardinal Semeraro: 'St. Paul VI a contemplative focused on dialogue.'" *Vatican News*, online at *vaticannews.va*, April 12, 2022.

Wawro Geoffrey, A Mad Catastrophe: The Outbreak of World War I and the Collapse of the Hapsburg Empire, Basic Books, New York, NY 2014.

Williams, Shannen Dee, *Subversive Habits: Black Catholic Nuns in the Long American Freedom Struggle*, Duke University Press, Durham, NC 2022.

Wilson, Michael, "The Holy Year of 1975," *The Catholic Hearld*, December 6, 1774, p.6, at *archive.catholichearld.co.uk*.

Winters, Michael Sean, "Remembering Paul VI." online at *ncronline. org/blogs*, August 6, 2013.

Zahn, Gordon C, "Pilgrim of Peace." in Paul VI: Critical Appraisals, James F. Andrews, Editor, Bruce Publishing 1970, pp.61-78.

Endnotes

Notes for Introduction

1   There were some 125 *coup* attempts, most but not all violent nor successful, during Paul VI's papacy from 1963-1978.

Notes for Chapter One

2   Jean Guitton (1968) *The Pope Speaks: Dialogues of Paul VI with Jean Guitton*, English Translation by Anne and Christopher Fremantle, Meredith Press, NY, p.281.

3   Discussed in more detail in Volume 1 is his unfortunate rejection of "pacifism" as "cowardly," and possessing of an unwillingness to do the hard work of negotiation or accept the sacrifices of a nonviolent struggle for justice.

4   These texts and his commitment to nonviolence are explored in detail in Volume 1.

5   Ali Parchami (2009) Hegemonic Peace and Empire: The Pax Romana, Britannica and Americana, Routledge Publishers, London.

6   See Adrian Goldsworthy (2017) *Pax Romana: War, Peace and Conquest in the Roman World*, Yale University Press, New Haven.

7   The bombing by the Allies of German and particularly Japanese population centers and heritage sites of Tokyo, Hiroshima and Nagasaki in 1945 to hasten the inevitable end of World War II was similarly intended to terrorize more than degrade the enemy war machine. See Chapter 7 of Volume 1.

8   It was not until 1935 with the passage of the National Labor Relations Act in the US that it became national policy to encourage collective bargaining by protecting employees' freedom of association, *i.e.*, to form unions.

9   It is impossible not to recall the attempts at ethnic cleansing in Ireland resulting from the oppressive conditions of British occupation during An Gorta Mór – "the Irish Famine." Between 1845 and 1851, British policies and practices resulted in the death of 1 million Irish and the emigration of another 1.5 million to North America and Britain. See Ruth-Ann Mellish Harris (1999) *The Great Famine and the Irish Diaspora in America*, University of Massachusetts Press, Amherst, MA; See also, beginning in 1857 with the *Indian Mutiny*, Britain's decades of reprisals resulting in the death of millions of Indians. Amaresh Mishra (2007) The War of Civilizations: India 1857. Rupa & Company, India.

10   The violence in Selma led to Johnson's "We Shall Overcome" speech to Congress and the passage of the most sweeping civil rights legislation since 1957 when, as Majority Leader of the Senate, Johnson was responsible for what to that time was the most sweeping civil rights legislation since the Civil Rights Act of 1875 during the presidency of Ulysses S. Grant. Reading the text of this speech for this book I prefer to refer to it as Johnson's "I want to be the president who..." speech: "I want to be the president who educated young children to the wonders of their world. I want to be the president who helped to feed the hungry and to prepare them to be taxpayers instead of tax eaters. I want to be the president who helped the poor to find their own way and who protected the right of every citizen to vote in every election. I want to be the president who helped to end hatred among his fellow men and who promoted love among the people of all races and all regions and all parties. I want to be the

president who helped to end war among the brothers of this earth." Lyndon Johnson, Joint Session of Congress, March 15, 1965, online at *voiceofdemocracy.umd.edu*. See also Doris Kearns Goodwin (2018) "Visionary Leadership: Lyndon Johnson and Civil Rights," pp.306-343 in *Leadership in Turbulent Times*, Simon & Schuster, New York, NY.

11   For a fascinating discussion of the threat of terrorism by far-right white nationalist groups in the US, See David D. Kirkpatrick (August 18, 2024) "Infiltering the Far Right." *The New Yorker*, online at *newyorker.com*. See also the Fresh Air interview of Kirpatrick by Tery Gross, "Why anti-fascist vigilantes are infiltrating far-right white nationalist groups." September 5, 2024, online at *npr.org*.

12   Online at *britannica.com/topic/The-Prince*.

13   George Washington (December 3, 1793), "Fifth Annual Message to Congress." Online at presidency.uscb.edu.

14   George Washington (December 3, 1793), "Fifth Annual Message to Congress." Online at *presidency.uscb.edu*.

15   Both Lincoln and his Secretary of State William H. Seward believed that the blessing of Emperor Maximillian I by Pius X in 1864 made him complicit in France and Spain's violation of the Monroe Doctrine. This, along with the pope's meeting with representatives of the Confederacy, were part of a string of events that led to the US breaking off all diplomatic relations with what at that time was States. The diplomatic consequences led as late as 1964 to Paul VI turning down an invitation by President Johnson to come to the US to meet. Paul VI explained to the president that as it was the US that cut off relations, he could not simply come to the US to meet the president. The pope did offer to meet Johnson at another location at the president's convenience. In the end Paul VI's 1965 visit to the UN gave them both the opportunity to meet as it "just so happened" that Johnson would be in New York 4 October for dinner with friends! See Chapter 6, Volume 1.

16   See *60-minutes*, March 19, 2023, online at *cbsnews.com*.

17   After three failed attempts the Empire finally successfully invaded Serbia with the help of German troops moved from the western front. See Geoffrey Wawro (2014) *A Mad Catastrophe: The Outbreak of World War I and the Collapse of the Habsburg Empire*, Basic Books, New York.

18   Italy joined the war in 1915 on the side of the Allies after secret negotiations in which Italy was promised territory in the event of an Allied Victory. The US entered in the war in 1917 after it had already reached a stalemate. Germans were starving due to a British naval blockade that persisted even after the armistice in November 1918. By March 1917 the Russian Czar Nicholas II had abdicated leading to civil war between the new Russian government's White Army and the Bolsheviks' Red Army under the leadership of Vladimir Lenin (1870 – 1924). With the victory of the Red Army Lenin made a separate peace with Germany in March 1918, just 8 months before Germany's complete surrender. By 1922 four socialist republics had united to form the Union of Soviet Socialist Republics. This later expanded to 15 republics making up the USSR until it fell in 1991.

19   Unlike Belgium, Russia's neighbor Belarus did allow Russian forces to invade Ukraine by way of that country on February 24, 2022.

20   *Si vis pace, bellum minaris* can be said to be not so much in service to security, but in

using threats to get what is wanted. Germany's threat to invade Belgium if the King did not agree to allow the Germans free passage on its way to France was not a bluff, as neither would be Hitler's threat to invade Czechoslovakia in 1938.

21   As of this writing treaties between the US and the Soviet Union have been rendered null by Russia.

Notes for Chapter Two

22   While I am not comfortable attributing to Paul VI a foundation beyond the traditional Judeo-Christian faith tradition, it is appropriate and important to acknowledge that the notion of peace that follows in this discussion mirrors the understanding of peace in Islam as described in the *Quran*. There are any number of academic references to which I could point, but one the reader may find of interest is the PBS interview of Professor Juan Cole at his 28 October 2016 lecture at the Library of Congress titled, "The Meaning of Peace in the Quran." Online at *pbs.org/wnet/religionandethics*.

23   Robin Young, "Former hostage negotiator on breaking contact with Hamas." Interview with Gershon Baskin, *WBUR*, November 2, 2023, at *wbur.org*.

24   No pun intended with reference to "shots" taken!

25   For an interesting discussion of the factors that lead to war, see Christopher Blattman (2022) "Why We Fight: The Roots of War and the Paths to Peace." Viking Press, NY.

26   Guitton (1968), p.280.

27   Guitton (1968), p. 281. He goes on to say he has been thinking about the idea that "development" can be considered a new term for peace: "I am pondering an encyclical on this central and vital theme, which I would like soon to place before all me." He did so in 1967 with his encyclical Populorum Progressio, "On the Progress of Peoples."

28   Online at *https://firmisrael.org/learn/the-meaning-of-shalom*.

29   From the Latin *cornu*, horn, and *copia*, abundance. In Greek mythology the original "horn of plenty" was that of the goat Amalthea who suckled the god Zeus.

30   It is worth noting that within Catholic Social thought justice is not and cannot be blind. "Blind justice" does not see the inherent inequalities in society rooted in ignorance and prejudice, social and economic status, historical circumstances, race, sexual orientation and gender-identity, physical disabilities, mental illness and the like. As a result, "blind justice" tends to favor those not encumbered by disparities, to the disadvantage of the disadvantaged. "Seeing" such inequalities, Catholic Social Thought calls on society to have a "preferential option for the poor," a principle articulated at the 1968 Synod of Latin American Bishops in Medellin, Colombia. Paul VI attended this Synod andfully embraced the concept that as "the Lord hears the cry of the poor" (Psalm 34,17), so too does justice require a degree of preferential consideration towards the poor and disadvantaged to assure their ability to fully share in the fruits of the common good. Citing the Prophet Sirach, 35,12-14: "The Lord is a God of justice, who knows no favorites. Though *not unduly partial toward the weak*." [emphasis added. See the Roman Lectionary, 13th Sunday in Ordinary Time Year C.] See also the Vatican II Pastoral Constitution *Gaudium et spes*, no.90 and the *Compendium of the Social Doctrine of the Church* (2004) Pontifical Council for Justice and Peace established by Paul VI in 1967, paragraphs 182-184. The need for an "open-eyed" justice is demonstrated throughout the writings and speeches of Paul

VI. The American philosopher John Rawls holds to a similar notion of justice, allowing for inequalities in the distribution of goods when done to "the greatest benefit of the least advantaged." See John Rawls (1999) *A Theory of Justice: Revised Edition*, Harvard University Press, Cambridge, MA, p. 266.

31   The supreme Greek god Zeus was often identified with the Roman god Jupiter: same god, different names.

32   The expression comes from outgoing President Dwight Eisenhower's farewell address to the nation delivered in a televised broadcast on January 17, 1961. See Bret Baier with Catherine Whitney (2017) Three Days in January: Dwight Eisenhower's Final Mission, Harper Collins, NY.

33   See "Former hostage negotiator on breaking with Hamas." Interview of Gershon Baskin by Robin Young, Hear & Now, September 4, 2024, online at wbur/hearandnow.org.

Notes for Chapter Three

34   Robert S. McNamara, (1996) In Retrospect: The Tragedy and Lessons of Vietnam, "Preface," Vintage Press Publishers, New York.

35   See chapter 6 of Volume 1.

36   Religious freedom was an important human rights issue for Paul VI, and he makes frequent reference to it in his writings and addresses. Although a point of controversy among conservatives, the reason for which much to the consternation of progressives the pope delayed promulgating the Declaration, the "Declaration on Religious Freedom," *Dignitatis Humanae*, was approved at the Vatican Council II by a vote of 2308 in favor and 70 opposed and promulgated by the pope December 8, 1965.

37   Honoring Mary as *Theotokos*, 'God-bearer,' dates to the Council of Ephesus in 413 and is the first Marian dogma adopted in Christianity. In the Eastern Church Mary was celebrated on September 8, "The Nativity of Mary, Mother of God." By the 7th century the West celebrated the "Maternity of the Blessed Virgin Mary" and the "Octave (8th) Day of the Nativity of the Lord" on January 1. By the 13th century January 1 had become the "Feast of the Circumcision of Christ." In 1970 Paul VI decreed that the "Solemnity of Mary" would supersede the celebration of the "Circumcision," returning New Year's Day to its original significance. People often miss that much of the liturgical reforms following Vatican II were matters of "restoration" rather than "innovation."

38   Clifford was also a presidential advisor to Harry Truman, John Kennedy, Lyndon Johnson, and Jimmy Carter.

39   An obvious exception is his first encyclical, *Ecclesia Suam*, "His (Christ's) Church." Modern pope's first encyclical can generally be characterized as a blueprint, outlining the new pope's vision of the Church and giving insight into what might be expected from his papacy. As such it will typically address variety of Church related issues. As noted previously it is in this encyclical that we find the term "dialogue," *dialogos*, used for the first time in an official Church document, it being used 14 times. Used with this frequency in his first encyclical is as clear an indication that can be found of the kind of papacy he would have: one of dialogue and conversation.

40   Oddly this most glaring error in the English translation has never been corrected.

41 See *Human Rights Innovators* (2016) Salem Press, pp.592-596.

42 This is in contrast to pope's historically avoiding being photographed with world leaders, with whom they rarely met in any case. See the account of President Wilson's visit with Benedict XV in 1919 in Chapter 5, Volume 1. See also Joseph McAuley (September 4, 2015) "When presidents and popes meet: Woodrow Wilson and Benedict XV." *America Magazine* online at *americamagazine.org*.

43 Pius IX named James Augustine Healy second bishop of Portland, Maine on September 12, 1875. Due to Healy's European ancestry he and his siblings were light-skinned passed for White in the US. See Albert S. Foley (1969) *Bishop Healy: Beloved Outcaste*, Amo Press, NY.

44 Perry is recognized as the first "openly black" bishop in the US. President Lyndon Johnson, who Perry is quoted as saying did more for civil rights than any president since Lincoln, publicly praised Paul VI for Perry's appointment.

45 For an excellent overview of the bishops Paul VI appointed in the US between 1973 and 1978, See John Alonzo Dick (2021) *Jean Jadot: Paul's Man in Washington*, AnotherVoice Publications, (no location given).

46 Cardinal Spellman was succeeded by the surprise appointment by Paul VI of New York's Auxiliary Bishop Terrance Cooke in 1968. Paul VI named Cooke cardinal the following year. Unlike either his predecessor or his immediate successor, Cardinal Archbishop John O'Connor named by John Paul II, Cooke preferred a low profile and sought to keep out of the media limelight. He was installed as archbishop on the same day as the assassination of the Rev. Dr. Martin Luther King, Jr, and went to Harlem that evening to plead for peace. In 1982 he broke with the majority of this fellow US bishops by opposing the position that "Nuclear deterrence as a national policy must be condemned as morally abhorrent because it's the excuse and justification for the continued possession and further development of nuclear weapons." Advocated by Paul VI nearly twenty years earlier, this statement was formally adopted by the US bishops in their pastoral letter, "The Challenge of Peace: God's Promise and Our Response." See Luke Hansen (May 3, 2013) "'The Challenge of Peace." *America Magazine* online at *americamagazine.org*. Like his predecessor Spellman, Cooke supported the Vietnam War effort. Unlike Spellman who held to a positive evaluation of nuclear deterrence, Cooke was suspicious of the idea, finding it to be merely "tolerable." See "Battling the Bomb in Church." *Time Magazine*, January 4, 1982, online at *time.com*.

47 https://www.history.com/topics/vietnam-war/vietnamization.

48 For reflections on forgiving See John Tuohey (2024) "The Art of Forgiving." In John Tuohey (2024) *Striving to be Perfect as the Heavenly Father is Perfect*, Christian Faith Publishing, Meadville, PA 2024, pp.15-32.

49 In 1973 Congress over-road Nixon's veto to pass *The War Powers Act*, limiting a president's authority as commander-in-chief to pursue military engagement without explicit Congressional approval.

50 As noted in Chapter 7, Volume 1, much of Germany's industrial infrastructure survived the Allies' bombing towards the end of the war. Stalin had much of this infrastructure dismantled and transported back to the Soviet Union, at the same time demanding reparations. US President Truman objected to the dismantling of Germany's infrastructure arguing that without the ability to recover their economy the Germans would not be able pay reparations. Stalin continued to help himself to Germany's

assets, but in the end was denied any reparations.

51 US Bureau of Labor Statistics (2017) "History of child labor in the United States." Online *bls.gov*; See also Laura Strickler (March 26, 2024) "Kids as young as 14 were found working at a Tennessee factory that makes lawn mower parts for John Deere and others." *NBC Nightly News*, online at *nbcnews.com*; Nicole Goodkind (July 30, 2023) "Illegal child labor is on the rise in a tight job market." *CNNBusiness Report*, online at *cnn.com*.

52 For a historical overview See George Black (March 16, 2010) "The Victims of Agent Orange the U.S. Has Never Acknowledged." *The New York Times*, online at *pulitzercenter.org*.

53 See James Willbanks (2013) Vietnam War Almanac: An In-Depth Guide to the Most Controversial Conflict in American History, Simon & Schuster, NY.

Notes for Chapter Four

54 See Rebecca Kesby (24 December 2012) "North Vietnam, 1972: The Christmas bombing of Hanoi." *BBC World Service*, online at *bb.com/news*; Marshall L. Michel, III (2001) *The Eleven Days of Christmas: America's Last Vietnam Battle*, Encounter Books, NY, and (2018) *Operation Linebacker II: The B-52's Are Sent to Hanoi*, Osprey Publishing, Clayton, NY.

55 Tom Wicker (21 December 1972) "Pope Deplores Bombing." *The New York Times*, p. 16. Several Italian papers reported that Paul VI had sent a secret papal note to Nixon protesting the bombing. This was denied by both the White House and the Vatican which stated such reports "lacked any foundation." See "Vatican 'Denies Pope Sent Plea to Nixon." *The New York Times*, p.1.

56 I had the opportunity to visit Srebrenica while in Bosnia & Herzegovina in 2006. To visit such sites is bone-chilling, as was my time in Sarajevo where it seems there are no longer any public parks, nearly all of them becoming the final resting place of the almost 14,000 killed during the Croation Siege between 1992 and 1995.

57 Some quotations use *desertum*, desert, rather than *solitudinem*, aloneness or solitude.

58 See Henry Kissinger (2003) *Ending the Vietnam War: A History of America's Involvement In and Extraction From the Vietnam War*. Simon & Schuster, NY.

59 See George Veith (2012) *Black April: The Fall of South Vietnam 1973-1975*, Encounter Books, NY, p.59.

60 For an interesting history of the role the future pope John Paul II played in obstructing the work of the Synod in preparing a final text, see Hebblewaite (1993), pp.626-27.

61 *Ibid*, p.651

62 Paul VI (August 23, 1968) *Address to the Campesinos of Colombia; Address for the Day of Development at Bogota*, Bogota, Columbia.

63 See "Pope Sets 1975 Holy Year." The New York Times, January 28, 1972, online at nytimes.com. The tradition of celebrating a Holy Year, also known as a Jubilee, began with Pope Boniface VIII in the year 1300. It was his intention that a Holy Year be celebrated by the Church every 100 years. Rooted in the Jewish practice of a Jubilee Year, a Holy Year is typically a time of reflection on the need for forgiveness

and reconciliation with God and one another. The timing for a Holy Year has evolved over time. It was changed from 100 to 50 years by Clement VI in 1343, to 33 years by Urban VI in 1390, and back to 50 by Nicholas V in 1450. In 1490 Paul II made the final change in timing, decreeing that what is referred to today as an "Ordinary" Holy Year be celebrated every 25 years. The Holy Year for which Pope Francis has call for 2025 will the 28th in the Church's history and will mark the 1700th anniversary of the Council of Nicaea in 325 from whence comes the Nicaean Creed which holds that the "Son" is "consubstantial" with the "Father." The relationship between the Father and the Son was one of great controversy in the 4th century. The practice of calling for an "Extraordinary" Holy Year between the Ordinary may be rooted in Pius XII's call for a "Marian Year" in 1954 following the overwhelming success of the Holy Year of 1950, the first to be broadcast throughout the world. The 1950 Holy Year also saw the pope's declaration of the dogma of the Assumption of the Blessed Virgin Mary. Similarly, Paul VI declared 1968 a "Year of Faith" to mark the 1,900th anniversary of the martyrdom of Saints Peter and Paul. A "Holy Year of Compostela," such as was celebrated in 1970, takes place on years in which the Feast of the Apostle St James falls on a Sunday. This tradition began with Pope Calistus II in 1122 upon his completing the Pilgrimage of Santiago de Compostela in Spain, a pilgrimage that has a variety of routes through southern Europe, each of which ends at the tomb of St James.

64 Pius V (1504-1572) is also known for the excommunication of Elizabeth I of England, as well as establishing the Feast of Our Lady of Victory, more commonly known as the Feast of Our Lady of the Rosary, after the naval victory of the Holy League over the fleet of the Ottman Empire October 7, 1571. The victory was credited to Our Lady of the Rosary. Lefebvre named his society after Pius X in recognition of his rejection of "modernism" and his reaffirmation of the sacraments celebrated in Latin according to the Roman Missal promulgated by Pius V as the only valid celebration of the sacraments in the Church. See also the relationship of Pius X with the US in Chapter 5, Volume 1.

65 Paul VI ordered the Society of Pius X disbanded in 1975 when Lefebvre ordained priests according to the 16th century Tridentine Rite. John XXIII modified this Rite in 1962. When Catholics attend the "Latin Mass" today, it is the "1962 Mass," not that of Council of Trent. John Paul II excommunicated the archbishop in 1988 after he ordained 4 bishops, again according to the Tridentine Rite, without the permission and over the objections of the pope.

66 John Paul II allowed the limited reintroduction of the 1962 Mass. Benedict XVI allowed the wholesale celebration of the 1962 Mass anytime and anywhere in 2007. Pope Franics has identified the celebration of the 1962 Tridentine Mass as divisive and rolled back Benedict XVI's permissions. Many bishops, my own included, have simply ignored the current pope's restrictions.

67 Paul VI was not alone in holding to the value of a celibate clergy. The "Decree on the Ministry and Life of Priests" of the Council, *Presbyterorum Ordinis*, holds that celibacy is an important sign that proclaims the Kingdom of God, although the Council did not rule out the possibility of a married clergy alongside the celibate clergy as seen in some Orthodox Churches. The 1971 Synod of Bishops affirmed the need to preserve celibacy in the Latin Church in its final document, *Ultimis Temporibus*, "The Image of the Priest." St John Paul II also affirmed the call to a celebate clergy in his 1992 Apostolic Exhortation, *Pastores dabo vobis*, "I will give you shepherds."

68 International Women's Year (IWY) was designated by the United Nations in 1975. Since that year March 8 has been celebrated as "International Women's Day." Paul

VI called for an end to discrimination of women based on their gender and called for respect for women's dignity and equality in 1971 in his Apostolic Letter, *Octogesima Adveniens*, at no. 13.

69   It I estimated that between 22,000 and 30,000 Argentinians were murdered or "disappeared" during this period. See "On 30th Anniversary of Argentine Coup: New Declassified Details on Repression and U.S. Support for Military Dictatorship." Online at nsarchive2.gwu.edu.

70   The Chapultepec Peace Accords that finally ended the civil war on January 16, 1992, were negotiated with the UN and Catholic Church acting as observers.

71   The Greensboro massacre was a deadly confrontation in which members of the Ku Klux Klan and the American Nazi Party shot and killed five participants in a "Death to the Klan" march organized by the Communist Workers Party.

72   The Commission was established in response to the practice in the 1950's of the practice by the Bureau of Indian Affairs and the Child Welfare League of America to choose mostly white adoptive parents for Indian children.

73   *See Reuters* (September 6, 2023) "British parliament approves disputed Northern Ireland amnesty bill." *Reuters*, online at *reuters.com*.

74   Geno Quiroz (April 3, 2023) "The Vietnam Veterans Memorial - By the Numbers." *National Infantry Museum*, online at *nationalinfantrymuesum.org*.

75   It may be recalled that Paul VI sent both President Kennedy and Nikita Khruschev telegrams of congratulations upon the signing of a treaty to limit nuclear testing in 1963. It would be another 15 years before more of these "moral weapons of peace" become a reality. At its 2024 Session, the General Assembly of the UN called for further protections of the environment, particularly space, from exposure to nuclear threats.

76   See also the letter to the Ephesians, 4,27-27: "If you are angry let it be without sin. Do not let the sun go down on your anger."

77   On November 27, 1970, the Pope was the target of an assassination attempt by Benjamín Mendoza y Amor Flores at Manila International Airport in the Philippines. It was only as he vested for Mass was it discovered he had been slightly wounded. Against the advice of his personal physician who feared the pope might become infected by the knife wound, the pope continued with his plans to celebrate Mass.

78   In Greek mythology, Sisyphus was king of Eophyra, now Corinth, who executed guests to show off his power. This angered the other gods who, as punishment, forced him to roll an immense boulder up a hill only to have it roll back down every time he reached the top. He would do this for all eternity.

79   The bombing of Tokyo took place March 9-10 March 1945. Codenamed "Operation Meetinghouse," the mission was carried out by 279 US Boeing B-29 Superfortress heavy bombers, destroying 16 square miles of civilian central Tokyo. In addition to the estimated more than 100,000 who lost their lives, over one million Japanese were left homeless. The Japanese called the bombing the "Night of Black Snow." See *britanica. com*.

80   Although from my own research it seems Paul VI never addressed the issue of demands for an "unconditional surrender" to end hostilities, such a demand might be said to be an example of this dissociation of life and peace of which the pope

speaks. Were the Japanese given the opportunity to "save face" in their surrender, as called for by some Republicans in Congress at the time, it doubtless would have come before the dropping of the atomic bombs and hundreds of thousands of lives may have been saved. The US government insisted that the "Instrument of Surrender" signed on the USS Missouri, September 2, 1945, include the words: "We hereby proclaim the unconditional surrender to the Allied Powers of the Japanese Imperial General Headquarters and of all Japanese armed forces and all armed forces under Japanese control wherever situated." Online at *archives.gov*. In his broadcast to the Japanese, Emperor Hirohito does not use the word surrender, stating simply that "We have decided to effect a settlement of the present situation by resorting to an extraordinary measure...the empire accepts the provisions of their (the Allies') joint declaration." (Potsdam Declaration of July 26 defining the terms for a Japanese surrender). Online at *en.wikipedia.org*. See Richard Samuels (August 3, 2020) "Why President Truman insisted on unconditional surrender." *MIT Center for International Studies*, online at *cis.mit.edu*.

81 "Or what king, going out to wage war against another king, will not sit down first and consider whether he is able with ten thousand to oppose the one who comes against him with twenty thousand? If he cannot, then, while the other is still far away, he sends a delegation and asks for terms of peace."

82 These acts against life will come close to him in 1978 when his boyhood friend, former Italian Prime Minister and Senator Aldo Moro, is kidnapped by the terrorist organization the Red Brigade in March of 1978. His bullet ridden body was found in the trunk of a Renault 4 on May 9, 1978. Paul VI presided at this funeral, after which he left for the papal retreat at Castle Gandolfo. Moro's funeral was Paul VI's last public appearance. He passed August 6. Moro's family did not attend the funeral in protest of the failure of the Italian government to negotiate with the terrorists. Nor were government officials invited to attend his burial. For his part, Paul VI did reach out publicly to the Red Brigade in an effort to attain Moro's release, even to offering his own life in exchange. The government responded angrily that the pope was interfering in state affairs and violating Italian policy of not negotiating with terrorists.

83 See Bill Chappell (August 17, 2017) "Psychologists Behind CIA 'Enhanced Interrogation' Program Settle Detainees' Lawsuit." Online at *npr.org*.

84 Elizabeth Cohen, John Bonfield, Justin Lape (August 28, 2021) "CNN EXCLUSIVE 'Something has to be done': After decades of near-silence from the CDC, the agency's director is speaking up about gun violence." *CNNHealth*, online at *cnn.com*.

85 Paul VI speaks in a somewhat prophet manner of the dangers of social media in his 1971 Apostolic Letter, *Octogesima Adveniens*, "On the 80th Anniversary of *Rerum Novarum*," at no. 20.

86 Some 240,000 Vietnamese and Cambodians fled to the US after the fall of Saigon in 1975. Over 400,000 Vietnamese "boat people" came to the US between 1977 and 1978.

87 The Council was established by Paul VI in 1967 in the spirit of *Gaudium et spes*, the "Pastoral Constitution on the Church in the Modern World" of Vatican II. Its specific charge is to tend to Vatican's relations with civil authorities. It is possible that, although he was aware in 1977 when he wrote this *Message* of the upcoming 1978 Special Session at the UN, he had not yet received an invitation to speak and thus does not refer to it here. Equally perhaps more possible is that in a spirit of humility he sought not to distract from his message by drawing attention to himself.

88 See Sarah N. Lynch (2023) "Hate crimes in US surge 11.6% in 2021, fueled by racial, ethnic bias." *Reuters*, online at *reuters.com*; Anti-Defamation League Press Release (December 11, 2023) "Unprecedented Rise in Antisemitic Incidents Post-Oct 7." Online at *adl.org*; New York Bar Association (2023) "Islamophobia Surges in the U.S. Due to Global and National Tensions." Online at nysba.org>*News Center*.

89 See Neil G. Ruiz, Carolyne Im, Ziyao Tian (2023) "Asian Americans and discrimination during the COVID-19 pandemic." Pew Research Center, online at *pewresearch.org*.

90 See Jessica M. Goldstein (October 29, 2021) "'Revenge porn' was already commonplace. The pandemic has made things even worse." *The Washington Post*, online at *thewashingtonpost.com*; Kara Kelleher (August 10, 22023) "Revenge Porn and Deep Fake Technology: The Latest Iteration of Online Abuse." Boston University School of Law, online at *sites.bu.edu*. The Federal Trade Commission has published advice for victims of revenge porn: "What to do if you are the target of revenge porn," May 10, 2021, at *consumers.ftc.gov*.

91 The presumably original Italian text speaks of "boys of the new time" - *ragazzi del tempo nuovo*. This is translated into French as *les enfants* (children), Portuguese as *crianças* (children), and Spanish as *e jovens* (young).

92 This is somewhat understandable as Paul VI was greatly out-traveled by his successor John Paul II whose papacy also lasted a dozen years longer. Whereas for example Paul VI was first pope to visit the US, John Paul II visited seven times. See CNA Staff (Apr 2, 2020) "Recalling Saint John Paul II's seven visits to the United States." *CAN*, online at *catholicnewsagency.com*.

93 See Real to Reel, a program of the Office of Communications of the Diocese of Springfield, MA, September 8, 2024, online at iobserve.org.

94 See Russell Shaw (April 8, 2018) "Benedict: The Forgotten Pope of Peace." *Our Sunday Visitor*, online at *oursundayvisitor.com*; Patrick Houlihan (August 3, 2017) "Benedict XV and the forgotten campaign to end World War I." *America Magazine*, online at *americamagazine.org*.

95 Paul VI was Beatified on October 19, 2014, and Canonized on October 14, 2018 by Pope Francis in St Peter's Square.

www.ingramcontent.com/pod-product-compliance
Lightning Source LLC
Chambersburg PA
CBHW031218120626
46545CB00003B/891